Wellesley College

The Legenda, Wellesley College

Wellesley College

The Legenda, Wellesley College

ISBN/EAN: 9783337156114

Printed in Europe, USA, Canada, Australia, Japan

Cover: Foto ©ninafisch / pixelio.de

More available books at **www.hansebooks.com**

THE LEGENDA

WELLESLEY COLLEGE

※

Published by the Senior Class

1894

To
Our Esteemed Ancestor
NOAH
This Legenda
is Dedicated with the Sympathetic Appreciation
of the
Class of '94

WE LOOK BEFORE AND AFTER

H. P. Drake.　L. B. Hardee.　The Roast　J. M. McGuire
　　　　　L. D. Smith.　S. H. Bixby　Academic Court　　　　M. W. Arcuson.
J. Williams.　　　　　　　　　　Advertising Agent
　　　　　M. H. Holmes　　L. P. Stipitz　Our Contributors　G. O. Edwards
　　　　　　　　　　　LEGENDA BOARD

"AND SIGH FOR WHAT IS NOT."

'94

Editor in Chief
Elizabeth Bailey Harden S.S.

Associate Editor
Helen Porter Cate Z.A.

Literary Editors
Mary Herbert Holmes Φ Σ
Grace Osborne Stewart T.L.E. Emily Daniel Senif Φ Σ

Art Editors
Chief
Sarah Hathaway Busby Igna
Associate
Emma Dugan Smith N. Jane Michaux T.L.E.

Business Editors
Elizabeth Lee LeClerc.
Marion Wharton Anderson S.S.

Preface.

WHEN the present Board first undertook the task of publishing a LEGENDA for the Class of '94, it was with a very definite idea of what a LEGENDA should be. We believed that it was primarily intended as a memory book for the students, wherein they might find the record of one year of College life; and that, like all memory books, it should deal principally with the lighter side of that life, — the pleasant experiences and amusing incidents, rather than the academic work and intellectual growth.

In our attempt to embody this idea in concrete form, we have, of course, met with many practical difficulties. One of the matters which have been most perplexing to us is that of personalities. When last spring the Class of '94 asked permission to publish a LEGENDA, it intimated its intention of excluding from the book all "personal grinds." These the present Board understood as meaning quotations with names or initials attached. In the course of our work the suggestion came to us that some might understand the term as meaning any allusion to personal peculiarities or weaknesses, whether in the form of quotations or otherwise. There had been, and is, not only in the Board, but among the students at large, so strong a sentiment against such allusions that it had not occurred to us to define our position in regard to them. They had been excluded as a matter of course. We were therefore perfectly willing to accept this new definition, which, though wider, really limited us less than the other, but we still considered ourselves bound by our first interpretation. With this exception, the whole matter of jokes has been left largely to our own discretion, and we have conscientiously tried to make our book satisfactory to both Faculty and students. We feel, therefore, that whatever our mistakes, they are not due to a lack of effort or of desire to please.

To those members of the Faculty who have aided us by their interest and sympathy, to our classmates of '94, and to other students who have rendered us assistance, we wish to extend our hearty thanks.

THE EDITORS.

The Founders of Wellesley.

THE beautiful story of the founding of Wellesley College is widely known. Sketches of Mr. Durant's remarkable career have not infrequently appeared in print. The present article aims to be supplemental rather than complete in itself, presenting somewhat fully, even at the expense of proportion, such data as are new. Moreover, previous accounts of the founding of Wellesley have, naturally enough, thrown the man's work and the man's life into the foreground. But Mr. Durant himself would not have had it so. None recognized more clearly than he the equal share borne by Mrs. Durant in all the sacrifice, thought, and labor which went to the making up of their great joint gift. In the will of 1870 occurs the emphatic sentence: "All the provisions in this will are made with the knowledge of my beloved wife, and to carry out our mutual plans and wishes." Wellesley has two founders. It is proposed in the present sketch to deal more particularly with the woman's life and work. Yet, in reality, the two histories are one. The separate life-streams early blend into a single river, known by music and by shining, by burdens borne and toils promoted, by happy countries watered, by fearless flow through sun and shadow to the eternal sea.

Mrs. Durant comes of a distinguished ancestry. Her mother's family bore the name of de Cazenove, honorably known in France for nearly a thousand years. The Huguenot branch withdrew from their native land at the Revocation of the Edict of Nantes, and established themselves in Geneva as bankers, dropping their titles as inconsistent with a business career. The deep religious feeling, innate in their Huguenot blood, no less than their financial station and authority, and their alliance with the ruling families of Geneva, soon gave the de Cazenoves a high influence in that "stronghold of religious liberty." Presently there were to be numbered among them not only successors to the office of Premier Syndic, and other powerful positions, but theologians of eminence. Mrs. Durant's grandfather, Antoine Charles Cazenove, was educated for a military career, but developed a taste for financiering. Going to England, he spent three years in the great banking house of the Cazenoves, then ranking with the largest bankers of London. He returned to Geneva on the eve of the Jacobin Revolution,—a miniature copy of the Reign of Terror. He himself, with his father and elder brother, were seized by the mob and thrown into prison, several hundred other leading citizens of Geneva suffering the same outrage. Not all of the Genevan aristocrats were so fortunate as the Cazenoves, who were acquitted and released, their reputation for goodness standing them in stead. Recognizing the precariousness of the times, and seeing the business of the city in confusion, they escaped to Holland, and thence to America. In Philadelphia the brothers met two sisters resident in that city, although natives of Baltimore, whom they afterwards married.

Mrs. Durant's grandmother was Hogan by name, of Scotch-Irish extraction, of American birth, of the Roman Catholic faith,—yielding in later life to the Protestant,—and of culture quite exceptional for the women of her day. The perfection of her French is a family tradition and example. She was an excellent Latin scholar, trained by her father, a teacher of eminence, and she was widely read in history and literature. Her husband, in facing the rude American conditions of a century ago, displayed the characteristic energy and enterprise of his family. This young Swiss refugee, in company with the Hon. Albert Gallatin, carried the first millstones across the Alleghanies, established flouring mills in the backwoods of Western Pennsylvania, and set up at Uniontown the first glassworks in this country. John Jacob Astor offered him partnership in his great fur venture; but Mr. Cazenove decided to try his fortunes as a shipping merchant, and would gladly have settled in Philadelphia, then the most considerable seaport of the United States. He was deterred, however, by the ravages of yellow fever there, his wife's younger brother being among the victims. The horror of this pestilence, as it raged throughout Philadelphia and New York at intervals during the last decade of the preceding century, may still be realized from the graphic descriptions of our first American novelist. Reading Charles Brockden Brown's "Arthur Mervyn," or "Ormond," one does not wonder that Mr. Cazenove sought a safer home in Alexandria, Virginia. The five sons and five daughters who in time enriched the household had the benefit of unusually good schools, kept, in part, by women from Massachusetts. Mrs. Durant's mother received her earlier education in these, but was sent, like her sisters, to Mme. Greleaud's boarding school in Philadelphia, for the accomplishments, while the brothers were despatched to Geneva. On a visit to Boston, in the winter of 1830, Miss Pauline Cazenove, singularly fair and winning, met Major Fowle, of the United States Army, and after some months consented to become his wife.

The Fowles of Watertown were no less interesting a family than the Cazenoves of Alexandria. Captain John Fowle, of English descent, had done good service in the War of the Revolution, which swept away most of his property, together with that of many another patriot. He was a man of lofty principles, "not only hating evil, but despising it." Captain

Fowle and his wife were reputed to be the handsomest bride and groom ever married in Newton; and their eight children, especially three of the daughters, were famed for extraordinary beauty. It is said that the father would sometimes steal out of the house and close the blinds to shelter his three Graces, as they sewed or read by the window, from the lingering looks of the passers-by. The standing toast through Middlesex County was the couplet, originating with Robert Treat Paine,—

>"To the fair of every town,
>And the Fowle of Watertown."

It was on many accounts a remarkable family, and one of peculiar interest to Wellesley College. The mother, Mary Cooke of Newton, was the daughter of Abigail Durant of Newton, from whom our founders take their name, and the sister of Susanna Cooke, who married Dr. Walter Hunnewell of Watertown, a Harvard graduate of 1787, these being the parents of our neighbor across Waban. The youngest Miss Fowle, the all-admired Adeline, married Mr. Samuel Welles, who came to be the leading American banker in Paris. Mr. Welles was born in Natick, and from his father's family the town of Wellesley received its name. A sister of Mr. Welles, the banker at Paris, married her first cousin, Arnold Welles of Boston; and the Welles estate, now enlarged and known as the Hunnewell estate, was inherited by their daughter, the late wife of the present proprietor.

But we must not let these fascinating Fowles fly away with us. Our concern is not with the beautiful Charlotte, who married Benjamin Wiggin, a successful American banker resident in London; nor with the gentle Maria, whose husband dreamed of the burning of Moscow at the very time when the conflagration was in progress; nor with the gallant young midshipman who fell in a duel with a British naval officer; nor with the graceful Eliza, who was said to be the only woman in Boston who could wear the long shawl elegantly; nor with the dazzling Adeline of Paris and Versailles, who, after the death of her husband, Mr. Welles the banker, married the Marquis de La Valette, a diplomat who rose under Napoleon III. to be Minister of Foreign Affairs, and, later, Ambassador to the Court of St. James. But there are two of this brilliant household group in whom Wellesley has every right to be interested: Harriet, most intellectual of all the children, a passionate lover of books, the soul of honor, impulsive and imperious, with an irresistible charm of her own, who became the mother of Mr. Durant; and John, the Major Fowle already mentioned, who became the father of Mrs. Durant.

Major Fowle was a man of two-score years when he made the acquaintance of Miss Cazenove. He had served in the War of 1812 on the New York frontier, and had taken part, with that illustrious corps known as Scott's Brigade, in the Niagara Campaign, remaining at the head of his company through the battle of Lundy's Lane, regardless of the wound he had received early in the action. He was much engaged, later, in the Indian wars on the frontier, in Arkansas and Minnesota. He was, like his father, a man of purest integrity, his nickname being Honest Jack. A strict disciplinarian, he was a commander who could command himself. Card-playing, for instance, had been an accustomed pastime at home, but as soon as he noted its demoralizing effect upon the soldiers in garrison, he would no longer allow it either to his men or to himself. He made it understood that he counted it an affront to be invited to a card party; and so resolute and consistent was his opposition to cards in garrison, that his superior officers were embarrassed to be discovered by him in a game. There was nothing petty in his nature. Even the keeping of accounts was given up by him, because he would not, as he said, "attach such consequence to a sixpence." Major Fowle exemplified the truth of the poet's words, "The bravest are the tenderest." He appears to have been quite the ideal lover, yet with a margin of courtesy and kindness for others than the sovereign lady. A sister of his betrothed refers to him, in a letter now yellowed with the years, as "the most thoughtful and considerate man for one in love we ever knew." And another of these treasured letters of long ago bears this enthusiastic testimony: "Sophia, Charlotte, and myself have unanimously agreed that since the creation of the world no *lover* ever was half so attentive and agreeable as the Major."

The marriage took place in May of 1831, and on the thirteenth of June in the following year was born, in Alexandria, the daughter without whom Wellesley College would never have been. She was a traveled baby. At the age of three months she journeyed on a pillow to Sault Ste. Marie, where Major Fowle was stationed. It was no easy trip in those early days. There was one little strip of railroad in Western New York, but apart from that and boats of one sort and another, the travelers had to depend on such rude vehicles as they could obtain over frightful roads with gaping holes, of which it was said you could lose a wagon in any one of them and never miss it.

The little party went to Fort Brady by the last boat of the fall, and were ordered to take their departure by the first boat of spring. The conditions of life there at the Sault were rough and primitive. Yet by the infrequent mails, carried on snowshoes or by dog teams, cheery letters went out from the brave young bride and her proud husband to the anxious people at home. The playful tone of the letter from which the following extracts are taken, a letter from Major Fowle to one of his wife's sisters, written in midwinter from the icebound fort, shows how warm and happy were those wedded hearts among the snows.

MY DEAR SISTER: I have been trying in vain to get my wife to give you some account of her sudden change as respects her opinions of the natives: therefore I must do it myself. A few days after our arrival here we walked out, to see and be seen. We came in sight of a number of wigwams; I proposed we should go and visit them. We went to the opening of one and found it occupied by a number of male Indians. After looking at them for a few moments we proceeded to another, and found it filled with females (Indians). Pauline entered into conversation with them in French, and I assisted with Indian; at last one of them said, in English, that she (Pauline) was very beautiful. This, of course, I agreed to, But it is astonishing what a change it has wrought. She never speaks of the Indians except she remarks what shameful treatment they have received from the whites, and, finally, by saying she feels for them, and they are a much-injured people, etc. . . . The two Paulines are in good health, and are quite contented with their situation. The little pet is very good-looking (the mother says, a great beauty), and looks, as all say, very much like her father. . . . Pauline has found her French of some use here. A Frenchman came one day to sell some partridges; he could not speak English, and she was called upon to make a bargain with him. The poor fellow was delighted to find she could speak French, and said he would come frequently to sell to her, and that his wife was very sick, and she would be much pleased to talk with her. I presume he thought his wife would be recovered by Pauline's conversation. As for making bargains, your sister is a very good Cazenove at it; our money here is bread tickets, say two and a quarter pounds, which cost us five cents.

In the spring of 1833, Major Fowle was ordered to Fort Dearborn, Chicago, to relieve troops that had been there during the Black Hawk War. At this time there were no regular chaplains in the army, and Major Fowle invited the home missionary, Mr. Jeremiah Porter, a great grandson of Jonathan Edwards, to accompany him. Mr. Porter had come out to Sault Ste. Marie the year before, and had organized a little Presbyterian church there. As the removal of the troops virtually removed his congregation, and as there was already a Baptist church at the Sault, where the Presbyterian remnant could be cared for, Mr. Porter accepted the Major's invitation. Many years after, the veteran missionary spoke with pleasure of the little child who brightened the deck of the small schooner that brought the troops to Fort Dearborn.

The new arrivals at Chicago, in this spring of 1833, found themselves on the edge of the flowering prairie in a straggling, waterside village, where two-story frame houses were just beginning to go up among the log cabins,—a village of barely three hundred inhabitants, including soldiers, traders of the American Fur Company, Indians, trappers, roughs; hard and wild characters, in the main, with a leaven of four "praying men" among them. These four gave delighted welcome to the newcomers; for the garrison embraced eighteen professing Christians, in addition to the missionary, and their coming was to the discouraged few like "the bursting out of the sun from the darkest clouds." The new command, well-drilled and well-principled, was, indeed, welcome to all; for these pioneer settlers knew what it was to suffer from disorderly, pilfering soldiers. The Major had been in Fort Dearborn before, and the excellence of his discipline was well known. "Now Major Fowle has come," said the people, "we shall be able to keep some chickens." The Major, although a regular attendant at Sunday service and at Bible class, was not enrolled upon the list of church members. Yet he reverenced his wife's Christian devotion, and worked with her for the promotion of Mr. Porter's labors, feeling that religion would be a sovereign agent for the regenerating of society in those frontier posts. On the first Sunday at Fort Dearborn the Major had the carpenter's shop swept out and rudely furnished with seats for service; and from this humble yet appropriate origin sprang the earliest church of Chicago.

While the infant church was making its way,—with its plain little house of worship out on the open prairie, its one silver sacramental cup, and its Sunday-school library that could be "comfortably carried in a silk handkerchief,"—Major Fowle had been promoted to West Point, as Instructor of Tactics and Commandant of the Corps of Cadets, winning here, as everywhere, universal confidence and esteem. It was said that the discipline had never been so good and so uniform, nor the cadets so well satisfied, as under Major Fowle's command. Here, at West Point, the little Pauline passed five sunny years, a baby brother and a baby sister claiming much of her childish attention. The sturdy tot, already possessed of more than her share of logic, was concerned that the tiny sister in long clothes did not go outdoors to play. "Mamma, if you don't send Annie out to walk, she'll never know what kind of an earth God has given her to walk on."

Upon Annie she promptly bestowed her "Mother Goose," finding that classic worthy "such an intolerable liar. I can't stand her; but Annie is too young to be hurt. She can just look at the pictures." Pauline was a budding financier, liking to save her pennies until they counted up to a goodly sum; while poor Annie, as the elder sister said disdainfully, "never could keep two pennies to rub against each other."

The little maiden was carefully trained in all womanly arts. Very neat and even are the many stitches in the pretty hussy laboriously fashioned as a gift for the handsome soldier papa, who had been promoted to the rank of lieutenant-colonel, and ordered to Florida, to take command of his regiment in the Seminole Indian Wars. The hussy was in his trunk when the Colonel, having placed his family temporarily in Alexandria, embarked at Cincinnati on the steamboat Moselle. The vessel was urged beyond her power, the boiler burst, and in the terrible disaster that filled the papers of the day, no manlier life was blotted out than that of Colonel Fowle. His wife, almost crushed by the shock and sorrow, began to lean upon her eldest child, the little daughter not yet six years of age, who was to be for more than half a century to come the widow's earthly strength and stay.

Mrs. Durant still remembers the sense of childish importance with which she led her toddling sister to the dressmaker, to see about their mourning dresses; for the mother, in the apathy of grief, left to this faithful five-year-old the choice and planning of the pitiful little frocks. The child's remarkable thoughtfulness and sense of responsibility had already been strikingly exemplified on the night of her father's death,—a catastrophe of which, in those days before the telegraph, the family still remained unconscious. A fire raged in the town; neighboring houses were in flames, and the children, caught up from their beds, were hurried away to a place of safety. But the sleepy little Pauline had a parting charge for her excited mother: "Mamma, don't forget papa's trunk with the valuable papers in it." This capable, small mortal also took it upon herself to look after her mother in traveling, as her father had always done, but with the reticence of childhood she confided to no one how sorely it galled her little soul to go on a half ticket. Her joy was great when, having passed her eighth birthday, the railroad officials could no longer brand her as "half a person."

The years in Alexandria were quiet, the natural mirthfulness of childhood subdued by the abiding shadow of sorrow. In less than two years from the father's death the baby boy slipped from human hold, and three years later the little sister followed. The one surviving child, early learning the great lesson of self-forgetfulness, was ever her mother's comforter. Visiting aunts in Boston during this period, little Pauline, eight years of age, came to know her cousin Henry, ten years her senior, and then a student in Harvard. The poet-hearted young collegian, handsome, as became his Fowle descent, won the friendship of the gentle child, whose appearance at the time he afterwards tenderly pictured in verse.

I well remember, cousin,	A pensive grace, dear cousin,
What you, perchance, forget;	And a thoughtful look was there,
That fair child, like a rosebud,	Like a loving girl's in reverie,
The dew upon it yet.	Or a mother's in her prayer;
That sweet face, like a rosebud	But when she played in childish glee,
Just opening to the air,	And gayly laughed the while,
With something of a maiden,	A beauty like a breaking wave
More of an angel there.	Beamed ever in her smile.

The little girl's education was carefully looked after. In addition to her mother's teaching, she attended for some time a private school in Alexandria, kept by a Mrs. Kingsford, an

English lady, wife of a Baptist clergyman. At home, meanwhile, she was thoroughly trained in music and drawing, fine sewing, elaborate cooking, and all the domestic arts.

"Oh, yes," a teasing uncle used to say, "we shan't keep her long. When she comes home from boarding school we'll put out a shingle to tell the world that within may be found the young lady who, at the age of thirteen, could make anything that man requires, from a shirt to a loaf of cake. We'll not be bothered with keeping her long."

The boarding school chosen was one of the leading institutions of the day,—a French establishment in New York City, under the charge of M. and Mme. Canda. The earnest-spirited young Southerner would have preferred Mount Holyoke Seminary, but here her mother stood firm. Mrs. Fowle had heard that at Mount Holyoke the custom prevailed of introducing the girls to foreign missionaries who came wife-hunting, and this precious, only daughter could not be so jeopardized.

Mrs. Durant gives amusing accounts of the conditions of life in this fashionable boarding school, where the studies were conducted for one half the day in English, and for the other in French. The girls slept in dormitories, the "long dormitory" holding thirty of the little iron beds. At the first bell the girls sprang to their feet with military promptitude, sleepily hurrying on stockings, slippers, and dressing gowns, turning back beds, opening windows, and betaking themselves with all inconvenient speed to the general dressing room above. Here some sixty toilets were simultaneously performed, the girls seeking shelter between the open doors of the tall presses that shared the wall space with the rows of washstands. Ablutions before these washstands were attended with thrilling perils. If water was spilled upon the floor, the culprit had to copy pages upon pages of French poetry. If the slop was exceptionally sloppy, the French poetry—for which one feels acutest sympathy—had to be learned by heart. After these appalling toilets the girls flocked back to the dormitories, made their beds, went to the schoolroom for prayers, and hungrily listened for the breakfast bell.

Here Mrs. Durant passed the years from fourteen to eighteen, making girlish friendships, and probably learning as much as if she rose later in the morning. The processional promenade along Broadway was not to her liking, and she was allowed to substitute for it exercise in one of the earliest gymnasiums of the city. The Sundays were usually spent with an aunt in Brooklyn, to whom Mrs. Fowle, who could not long be absent from her daughter, often came for extended visits. There were occasional trips to Boston, too, bringing renewal of friendshid between the winsome schoolgirl and the brilliant, though reluctant apprentice to the law.

Mr. Durant had had, as a child, an insatiate love of reading. To lie on the sofa with a book was his delight, in which his parents acquiesced as the surest recipe for keeping their wide-awake boy out of mischief. He was a chivalrous little fellow, with romantic day dreams of his own, and in his boyhood an ambitious class student. But his Harvard education was largely acquired in the college library. "I studied immensely the last part of the time I was in Cambridge," he said, "and to great advantage. I had but few recitations, and saw scarcely anyone, so that I had plenty of time." Greek was a favorite study with him, but he devoted much attention to English, reading widely and deeply, and practicing himself in verse composition, as well as prose. He dreaded the law, being haunted by "that horrid dream of a legal profession." But after graduation from Harvard, at nineteen, he dutifully entered the law office of his father, Mr. William Smith, in Lowell, the family having removed thither from Hanover, New Hampshire, where Mr. Durant was born. Writing to a friend, the young graduate said: "I shall study law for the present, to oblige father; he is in some trouble, and I wish to make him as happy as possible. The future course of my life is undetermined, except that all shall yield to holy poetry. Indeed, it is a sacred duty. I have begun studying law; don't be afraid, however, that I intend to give up poetry. I shall always be a worshiper of that divinity, and I hope in a few years to be able to give up everything and be a priest in her temple."

One year of Blackstone called out this second confidence: "I have not written any poetry this whole summer. Old Mrs. Themis says that I shall not visit any more at the Miss Muses. I'll see the old catamaran hanged, though, but what I will, and I'll write a sonnet to my old shoe, directly, out of mere desperation. Pity and sympathize with me."

After eighteen months of such tyrannical law studies, Mr. Durant, in the spring of 1843, his twenty-first birthday hardly passed, was admitted to the bar. Henceforth there was little opportunity for poetry. His legal practice ruthlessly swept him into the current of practical affairs. "It was impossible," he wrote, "to imagine a school better fitted than this to develop any latent talent for business, and for breaking up any tendency toward literary tastes."

However incompatible legal pursuits may be with writing poetry, they fortunately admit of living poetry. But before love in its fullness should reawaken the benumbed spirit of song in the young lawyer's heart, several years were yet to intervene. For him these were years of intense mental activity. "His genius, which many believed to be of the highest order, was primarily a genius for labor." He removed to Boston, establishing his law office in the northeast corner of the old State House, and changing his name, because another Henry W. Smith was already practicing law in Boston, to Henry Fowle Durant. In Boston his law partner was Mr. Joseph Bell, brother-in-law of Rufus Choate, in Lowell his father, and his law business was divided between Suffolk and Middlesex Counties. Rufus Choate began to employ him as junior counsel,—an association of great and varied benefit to the younger man, who spared no toil to gain the phenomenal success which soon was his. "At the Middlesex bar he was always in his place, and always alert. He had few associates, every hour of his time being absorbed by his profession. He apparently took little notice of current questions of the day. Sometimes he was genial, and sometimes icy, often preoccupied, absorbed, intense, and perhaps imperious, mysteriously making up a case, presenting it, and then retiring, only to reappear when he had a new case to win; never really happy unless undertaking some work of surpassing difficulty, which might fully tax all his powers. It was said of him that he was more frequently employed in what were considered desperate cases than any other lawyer of his time. An eminent man in his profession said of him that 'he was the most persistent, persistent, persistent man he ever saw.'"

Meanwhile, his destined wife was ripening in every womanly grace. After her four years at boarding school were ended, she visited, with her mother, Trenton Falls, Niagara Falls, and Sharon. Here Mrs. Fowle had a hemorrhage, which determined them on spending the next two winters in the south of Europe. The first of these was passed with Mrs. Wiggin, at the villa of the Marquise de La Valette, in Southern France, and the second in Rome, Florence, and Naples, their summer travels extending into Switzerland, England, and Scotland. On their return home, Mr Durant, all engrossed with his profession as his associates supposed him to be, found time to meet them in New York. But his beautiful cousin passed the following winter south, in Augusta, Mobile, and New Orleans, and it was not until the latter days of November, 1853, that his soul, long turned to hers,—so his poems whispered,—

"Like a pilgrim to his shrine,"

knew its devotion accepted.

There was one more winter of separation, in which blithest, sweetest love songs winged their way from the lawyer's desk, where the tedious writs and briefs must have marveled at them, to Washington and Alexandria. But Mr. Durant had already a practice of ten thousand dollars a year, and the marriage was not delayed. In the following May, her mother's wedding month, this younger Pauline wore the bridal veil. Then came household happiness almost unalloyed, love, as the lover had prophesied, deepening with the years.

To Pauline.

Tell me not that love is fleeting,	Every day our love grows dearer,
That its brightness fades away;	Every night love's holy prayer
While the hearts within us beating	Makes the lofty sky seem nearer,
Promise love and truth for aye.	While the star of love is there.

> Love is still a child immortal,
> And his wings will soon expand,
> As we near the shadowy portal
> To that other promised land.
>
> Whether born in joy or sorrow,
> Whether crowned with thorns or flowers,
> Love looks forward to a morrow
> In a brighter world than ours.
>
> Past the sleep that knows no waking,
> Past the night that turns to day.
> There the dawn of love is breaking.
> There the shadows pass away.

Their Boston home was located, first, on the corner of Bowdoin and Allston Streets. In 1860 they removed to 77 Mt. Vernon Street, and in 1868 to Mrs. Durant's present residence, 30 Marlborough Street. The Wellesley estate was purchased the year after the marriage, and here the summers were spent in what is now known as the farmhouse. The young wife delighted in putting to use her domestic accomplishments. In these first summers at Wellesley she used herself to skim every pan of milk that came into the house, and make all the preserves and delicacies. She loved the grounds, and knew each tree by name. She was interested in raising fowls, and was so proud of nineteen baby turkeys, of a choice breed from Brandywine, that on a stormy night she and her husband both rose to the rescue of that precious brood. While Mr. Durant groped about in the thunderstorm, and hunted down, by the flashes of lightning, one affrighted turkeykin after another, until all the nineteen had been caught, Mrs. Durant made a fire in the kitchen stove, and tenderly taking each little gobbler as it was triumphantly presented by its dripping deliverer, put a drop of wine down its throat and deposited it in a basket in the oven, to dream cozily of Thanksgiving Day until it had recovered from its chill.

In the spring of 1855 great joy befell them in the birth of their only son, Henry Fowle Durant, Jr., and in the fall of 1857 a little Pauline Cazenove gladdened the household for a brief six weeks. The death of this infant was a poignant sorrow to the parents. Added to her maternal mourning was Mrs. Durant's keen disappointment that the pain of this loss did not turn her husband's heart to the Divine comforter. She had herself united with the Presbyterian church when a schoolgirl, in 1847, and was as unswerving in her Christian faith as she had ever been untiring in Christian service. Mr. Durant was a man of essentially religious nature. An extract from a letter written soon after his twenty-first birthday to a college friend is evidence enough of this, although other evidence, as his admiration for the Bible, or his pleasure in the church service, is not wanting. The letter runs:—

DEAREST HOLKER: I have but one word to write to you, and that is immortality. It is all I have learned for a year, and yet the time has been well spent. Henceforward there is nothing to fear in life. It came at the right time. Sick with labor and sorrow, in the cold winter night I stood by the great river, and from the wind among the treetops, and the bright stars, and the ceaseless voice of the waters, I heard the one word that gives life and strength, and from that time there is no need of sorrow or of weariness.

But with all his delicate instincts and noble aspirations, Mr. Durant had never yielded his will to God. He now sought escape from sorrow in the rapid rereading of the Waverley novels, replying to his wife's entreaties, "You must take your medicine in your way, and I must take mine in mine."

The father and mother, thus bereaved, lavished their love all the more abundantly upon their boy, an exquisite child of rare intellectual promise. Generous-hearted, affectionate, and fearless, inheriting the beauty and high spirit of his parents, this cherished son,

> "The hyacinthine boy, for whom
> Morn well might break and April bloom,—
> The gracious boy, who did adorn
> The world whereinto he was born,"

delighted his father's pride and stimulated his father's ambition, giving impetus to every toil and significance to all the future. He was his mother's close companion and daily joy. Before her his childish heart lay as an open volume, white of leaf. A friend wrote: "One incident which occurred only a few days before he was taken ill, I recall at this moment. Willie, of whom he was very fond, said, 'Harry, I'll tell you something if you wont tell anybody.' 'I'll tell my mamma,' answered the dear child; 'I always tell my mamma everything I know.'"

In his ninth year Harry suddenly sickened and died, and through that illness and that death the father's life was consecrated to God. This was the mother's consolation,—a joy even deeper than her unutterable sorrow. Ever sacred to Wellesley College must be the prayer written at this time by Mr. Durant for their use together, and daily repeated by them for many years :—

"O Eternal and Holy Jesus, because we humbly believe that out of thy great and tender mercy toward us thy servants, thou hast not been willing to spare to us the life of our beloved boy, but hast taken him as a little lamb gently up in thine arms to bear him to sweet and sacred pastures in thine own Emmanuel's land, therefore we do beseech thee to make this great sorrow to be to us a means of salvation, a fountain of immortal hopes and consolations.

Grant to us, in our humility, the abiding faith that this our son is not dead, but is alive again; that he hath not been taken away from us, but has gone his way before to the Celestial City, where we, too, may soon enter in to be led by him to thy feet, if we through our sincere repentance and by thy saving grace may at last win pardon and remission of our sins. We beseech thee, also, O Lord, that it may not be counted as a sin in us if we, in all humility and lowliness of heart, do now in our affliction cherish the faith that this, our dearly beloved son, has fulfilled the mission given to him by his Father in Heaven, by teaching to us, his earthly parents, through his death, the worthlessness and vanity of all that this world can give or take away, and, that mission ended, he, innocent and pure, has gone before us to lead us in the way of salvation. We pray thee also, O Lord, that through thy holy blessing we may, each day that we live in this world, cherish always the sweet and precious memory of this our beloved and only son; and grant of thy most merciful kindness that our love for him and his love for us, so true and so tender that it never knew any change or shadow of turning, may become a holy and blessed means of leading us from sin, and all the temptations and sorrows and vanities of this evil world, to the only life which is eternal and that fadeth not away.

"O Christ, teach us to say, the Lord gave, and the Lord taketh away; blessed be the name of the Lord. And, oh, Lord Jesus, because thou hast also said, out of the great tenderness of thy divine love, 'Suffer the little children to come unto me, and forbid them not, for of such is the kingdom of God,' we do, therefore, beseech thee that through thy abiding mercy we may receive the Kingdom of Heaven as little children, and may one day stand at thy feet with this our departed child, all our sins forgiven through our sincere repentance, by the mystery of thy redeeming blood and pardoning grace; there with him, and with our little daughter, who went before, to worship the Father, the Son, and the Holy Ghost, forever and forever."

A few months after the child's death, Mr. Durant, who, fame and fortune and the highest legal honors at his command, had quitted the bar, and entered, this layman of "seraphic speech," into the preaching of the gospel, said to his wife:—

"Wouldn't you like to consecrate these Wellesley grounds, this place that was to have been Harry's home, to some special work for God?"

On such high foundation stands Wellesley College. From such a costly loss arose our gain. We know the story of the deciding, the planning, the building, the opening, the organizing,—of all the splendid energies poured into the work by brilliant brain, and fervent heart, and unconquerable will. At last the dream of youth came true. At last the baffled poet wrought his great life poem, but out of materials richer than words. Once a year we are hushed in chapel to hear again the inspiring history and receive the solemn message of that founder who is no longer in our sight. But the beloved founder who is yet with us hides herself so modestly from recognition and from praise, that of her we know far less than we would. Yet we cannot be altogether unaware of the ceaseless benevolence of that most fruitful life. Trained in childhood by her mother's precept and example to enrich the gift of money by the gift of service, the little hands accustomed to sewing for the poor, the little voice to reading for the blind, Mrs. Durant in womanhood has borne rich harvest of good seed. When a girl in Europe, surrounded by gayeties, she made opportunity for visiting prisons and other refuges of sin and misery. And so, after their home was left unto them desolate, while the husband held great audiences enthralled by his impassioned preaching, the wife was binding up broken hearts in Dedham Asylum, in Bridgewater Workhouse, in Boston Jail. For seven years Mrs. Durant served on the Advisory Board of the Massachusetts Prison Commission. For twenty-five years she has been—and always by unanimous election—the President of the Board of Managers of the Boston Young Women's Christian Association. To this latter institution, as to Mount Holyoke, she has given generously of her substance.

Her specific gifts to Wellesley it is impossible to completely enumerate. She has forgotten, and no one else ever knew. So long as Mr. Durant was living, husband and wife were one and inseparable in service and donation. But since his death, while it has been obvious that she spends herself unsparingly in college cares, adding many of his functions to her own, a continuous flow of benefits, almost unperceived, has come to Wellesley from her open hand. Freeman Cottage has arisen, furnished and adorned; Waban Cottage has been enlarged, the Eliot established; ice houses have been built, and homes for the college workmen. Valuable tracts of land have been purchased. Town water has been brought into the outlying halls and buildings, the gymnasium has been equipped, the chapel, kitchen, and laundry supplied with ventilating apparatus. The Botanical department, the Zoölogical museum, the art collections have received varied and valuable contributions. The beautiful Jarvis collection of laces, embroideries, and stuffs has been placed in the Farnsworth School of Art. Precious engravings have slipped themselves into the Shakespeare cabinet. A fine bronze placque in honor of Prof. Horsford has been hung in the library. Cut flowers and plants from Mrs. Durant's conservatory have continually found their way to studio and botany class, to student frolic and academic festival.

But these and such as these, representing although they do thousands upon thousands of dollars, are the least of Mrs. Durant's gifts to the College. She gives us an abiding example of magnanimous character, of Christian consecration. We know her for a shining spirit.

She lavishes her very life in labor of hand and brain for Wellesley, even as her husband lavished his. To this work of God she gives herself, and she gave him. It was a woman's prayer that blossomed in every Christian deed of his. I venture to quote from a personal letter written by Mrs. Durant this spring of '94.

"I gave myself to the Lord, Aug. 23, 1847, and have ever tried to consecrate to Him all He has given me since. This dedication of myself was a distinct act, and when God gave me the love of Henry F. Durant's soul, I gave that to Him also."

KATHARINE LEE BATES.

HELEN ALMIRA SHAFER, M.A., Ph.D.

Glimpses of Miss Shafer.

IN MEMORIAM.

AS I sit and ponder how it is possible for me to attempt even a very superficial record for the '94 LEGENDA of one whose going away has marked the year 1894 with a long shadow for each Wellesley student, there are two or three pictures which rise to my mind, and which may not be inappropriate to these pages.

To the "old girls" there is one spot in the great College dining room which presents a series of memory pictures. In each one a tall, dignified woman, with an interested, sympathetic face, is the center. The table in the northwest corner was the one long known as "Miss Shafer's table." Those who have been her "table girls" realized how fully the dinner hour was a period of relaxation. Then was the time to tell all the fun and frolic, and many were the good times then and there planned. Each was sure of an appreciative listener; each felt sure that behind the smiles was an unusually keen and true sense of justice. From that sense came the confidence in the wisdom of any decision which Miss Shafer might make. The fact that sometimes the fun narrated was not approved of, hindered in no measure the account of the next "lark." One never feared that her approval might be warped by her former disapproval, especially if she had the good fortune to hear, "You girls did me so much good; your fun and frolic was such a relief after the work of the day." At the table the frail health of Miss Shafer was more apparent, perhaps, than anywhere else. The carefully regulated diet, the fear of chill air, the love for all that was dainty in china and service, were part of a delicate constitution.

To a few of these "table girls" came the privilege of gathering for an hour after dinner one day in the week in Miss Shafer's room, while she read aloud. To some of them, "Little Lord Fauntleroy" will always possess an especial charm because introduced by Miss Shafer's appreciative voice. In each memory picture the forms of the girls who played a part in these "homey" times fade into dimness, and the central figure stands forth, serene and dignified, full of interest and sympathy, inspiring and begetting confidence—one to be *trusted*.

Because of this knowledge of interest, sympathy, and justice, other memory pictures now exist. To all Wellesley girls the President's office is familiar. The editors of the first

LEGENDA have only the pleasantest recollections of that office. Whether the sun streamed through the long windows, flooding all the room with sunshine, as it has a way of doing, or the rain beat against the windowpane, the recollections are always happy. From the first application from the Class of '89 for the issue of a college annual, Miss Shafer was always full of interest. Throughout its whole career she gave her hearty support. In each detail she was interested. When she felt unable to give her consent to the insertion of some feature, she always gave her reasons as fully as she could. Occasionally she would say, "Personally I should have no objection to that, but it does not seem wise to introduce it; I would not." This warm interest has been extended through all the vicissitudes of the LEGENDA.

There can be but few, if any, of the Wellesley students who knew Miss Shafer as President, who have not had similar experiences in that little office. Perhaps sometimes it would seem that Miss Shafer saw manifold objections, and that the petitioner would go away with a feeling that her request would not be granted, only to find that it was granted more fully and completely than she had hoped. Perhaps she would go away feeling angry because her request was refused. I think that could not have happened often, and I have yet to find the Wellesley student who could not and would not say, "I can always feel sure of the fairness of Miss Shafer's decision." Again and again have Wellesley students said, "She treats us like women, and knows that we are reasoning beings."

There is another glimpse which is a most familiar one. It is that of Miss Shafer in her own parlor at Norumbega, graceful, cordial. Then, more than at any other time, in long, friendly talks did her absolute absorption in the College come out. It was her life. She seemed to have scarcely a thought beside it. She was so eager to develop it from all sides. Wellesley's interests were her own. Often she has said, "I feel that one of Wellesley's strongest points is in her alumnæ." And once more, because of this confidence, the alumnæ, as when students, were spurred to do their best, were filled with loyalty for their Alma Mater. Miss Shafer always welcomed with cordiality any plan or suggestion which an alumna might have for any department of college life and work. An alumna could not but feel that she had come into special privileges in knowing how actively, wisely, and progressively Miss Shafer was engaged in pushing the interests of the College. It could not but fill one with amazement to see the manifold threads which so delicate a woman could hold and control. That they wore upon her more than any one was conscious is now apparent. Her delight in the tales and jokes of which her keen sense of humor made her the more appreciative, was no doubt enhanced by a desire for relief from the routine of her daily life. It was almost pathetic at times. Even more touching was the feeling in these later years that she could not know the girls; that she did not have their friendship and companionship as she had done.

Lonely and isolated her life seemed at times. At first thought such a saying in connection with the life of a college president appears strange. On reflection it becomes true.

The pen tributes which appeared in the February number of the *Wellesley Magazine* presented so varied a view of Miss Shafer, they bear the impress of so much sympathy and love, that one finds she is but repeating what has been already better said. I can bear witness only as a Wellesley student and alumna, but there are certain characteristics of Miss Shafer which have impressed all.

Miss Shafer's keen sense of humor, which enabled her to enter more fully into the life of the students, her appreciation of other sides of a question, her ready insight into character, her charity, enabled her to call forth the best in those with whom she came in contact. As regards herself, she was a true heroine. Many another woman with her frail physique would have given up the struggle. She kept on bravely to the end, and passed into the larger life from the midst of her duties here. With her, duty was supreme, but duty transcending itself and becoming privilege. This sense of duty did not crowd upon her and overwhelm her in details. She was always thorough, but she did not lose her equilibrium. No matter what the pressure of work, she never expressed "hurry" in her manner. There was always a poise, a self-control. This was all a part of her singular sincerity, simplicity, and directness of character. It all comes back to her well-nigh complete loss of self.

Wellesley, past, present, and future, has deep cause of gratitude toward Miss Shafer. Although but just begun, according to her plans, she had already brought the inner organization of the College to a high state of perfection. From the intellectual side, many new courses were introduced under her administration. The crowning point of it all is the curriculum, but newly introduced, which places Wellesley in the front rank of progressive American colleges, and opens wide opportunities. Nor was she unmindful of the physical side. Her constant plea was for a new gymnasium, her constant desire for the health of the students. With all phases of the social life of the students she had sympathy likewise. She recommended to the Trustees the representation of alumnæ on their Board. That recommendation has now been adopted. Certainly these are all indicative of the growth of the College under Miss Shafer's administration, and of the influence which she wielded. But the most potent influence is that of her own life. If I should try to formulate an expression of that life in brief, I should say that in her relation to the students there was perfect justness; as regards her own position, a passion for duty; as regards her character, simplicity, sincerity, and selflessness. Such was the woman to whom we delight to do honor, however feebly. Such the woman whose loss we mourn. Such the woman for whose entrance into Light we rejoice.

CAROLINE L. WILLIAMSON, '89.

EBEN N. HORSFORD, M.A.
ALEXANDER McKENZIE, D.D.   PHILLIPS BROOKS, D.D.

Officers of
Government and
Instruction.

Board of Trustees.

ALEXANDER McKENZIE	Cambridge.
President of the Board.	
*RUFUS S. FROST	Chelsea.
Vice President.	
MRS. PAULINE A. DURANT	Wellesley.
Secretary and Treasurer.	
WILLIAM CLAFLIN, LL.D.	Boston.
WILLIAM F. WARREN, S.T.D., LL.D.	President of Boston University.
ALVAH HOVEY, D.D., LL.D.	President of Newton Theological Seminary.
WILLIAM H. WILLCOX, D.D., LL.D.	Malden.
DWIGHT L. MOODY	Northfield.
ELISHA S. CONVERSE	Malden.
MARY B. CLAFLIN	Boston.
MARTHA W. WILKINSON	Cambridge.
*WILLIAM S. HOUGHTON	Boston.
EUSTACE C. FITZ	Boston.
LILIAN HORSFORD	Cambridge.
ALICE FREEMAN-PALMER, Ph.D., L.H.D.	Cambridge.
HORACE E. SCUDDER, B.A.	Cambridge.
MARION PELTON GUILD, B.A.	West Roxbury.
EDWIN HALE ABBOT, M.A.	Cambridge.
WILLIAM LAWRENCE	Bishop of Massachusetts.
*HELEN A. SHAFER, M.A., Ph.D.	President of Wellesley College.

* Deceased.

Pedagogus Wellesleyanus.

The following observations concerning the appearance and habits of this exquisite little creature have been made expressly for LEGENDA students.

GENUS	Homo.
SUB-GENUS	Pedagogus.
SPECIES	Wellesleyanus.

GENERAL DESCRIPTION.

The Pedagogus Wellesleyanus is a familiar sight upon the campus, and owing to its accessibility will serve admirably as a type of the sub-genus. It ranges from five to six feet in height, and is in outward appearance a bilaterally symmetrical animal. The genus Homo among Vertebrates agrees with the group Mollusca among Invertebrates, in that the members of both groups are enveloped in mantles. The mantle of the Pedagogus Wellesleyanus is frequently very complex, and difficult of comprehension. It adapts itself to the mode of life and character of the animal. Lavender, green, and bright blue mantles have been observed, but the prevailing color is a subdued or mottled brown. The scientific investigation of individuals of this species requires great delicacy of manipulation, for as a rule the Pedagogi are very sensitive to touch. Though the outward appearance is symmetrical, the animal itself is rarely so. The species is generally marked by an unusual development of certain powers and the more or less complete atrophy of others; the direction of growth varies, and the result is a collection of highly individualized units. All possess a backbone of varying degrees of hardness, most possess a stern-um, some few are blessed with a humor-us. According to some authorities occasional specimens are cold-blooded.[*]

DISCUSSION OF THE SUB-GENUS.

The Pedagogi as a rule are sedentary in habit. Some varieties are wild, and must be approached in their native lairs with great circumspection. Others have been domesticated, and are in demand for household pets. Much might be written about individual eccentricities, but that branch of the subject forms a complete course of study in itself. Besides variations due to habit, we observe in some peculiarities which are marks of old family precedents, which have been transmitted to them from ancestors living in remote geologic times.

---
[*] A leading authority of to-day denies this.

DEVELOPMENT.

The young Pedagogus begins his career in a very undeveloped condition, and passes through several metamorphoses before reaching the adult stage. One of the most curious of the larval forms, called Studentus, is distinguished by a capacity for fun and a wonderful agility in evading regulations. When the organ of authority becomes functional, however, these may gradually atrophy, even the memory of them finally disappearing. An early stage in the development is depicted in the accompanying diagram, and the enormous capacity for mental development may be observed by a comparison of the accompanying specimen of the mental attainments of a Pedagogus Wellesleyanus at the age of ten with a production at the age of (?).

1. To a Class in Scriptural Geography.

    We are in a pleasant land,—
    'Tis the land of Palestine:
    We're a happy, youthful band,
    In the land of Palestine.

    And we study of our land,—
    'Tis the land of Palestine:
    We are but a little band,
    In the land of Palestine.

2. The resemblance between phylogenesis and the ontogenesis, whether of an organ or of an organism, is diminished and to an extent vitiated by the introduction of cenogenesis. Certain characters in the gonangia of the blastostyles of certain calyptoblastia will immediately occur to the mind as clearly illustrating this principle.

HELEN A. SHAFER, M.A., Ph.D., President.

Department of Latin.

FRANCES ELLEN LORD . *Professor.*
ADDIE BELLE HAWES, B.A., Oberlin . . *Instructor.*
ESTHER BOISE VAN DEMAN, A.M., Michigan University *Instructor.*

Department of Greek.

ANGIE CLARA CHAPIN, B.A., Michigan University *Professor of Greek Language and Literature.*
JULIA JOSEPHINE IRVINE, M.A., Cornell University *Professor.*
ANNIE SYBIL MONTAGUE, M.A., Wellesley College *Associate Professor.*
EDITH SOUTHER TUFTS, B.A., Wellesley College *Instructor.*

Department of German.

CARLA WENCKEBACH *Professor of German Language, Lecturer on Pedagogics.*
MARGARETHE MÜLLER *Instructor.*
ELSBETH MÜLLER . . *Instructor.*
LOUISE CLARA MARIA HAUERMEYER *Instructor.*
ANNA BEINHORN . *Instructor.*

(Died January 25, 1894.)

Department of French.

ADELINE PELLISSIER, B.S., Académie de Paris . . . *Acting Professor.*
AMÉLIE TOURNIER, B.E., Académie de Basançon . . *Instructor.*
JULIE FÉLICIE MARIE CLAVEL, B.S., Faculté de Toulouse *Instructor.*

Department of Philology.

HELEN L. WEBSTER, Ph.D., Zurich University, Switzerland . *Professor.*

Department of Italian.

MARGARET HASTINGS JACKSON . . *Instructor.*

Department of Botany.

SUSAN M. HALLOWELL, M.A., Colby University *Professor.*
CLARA EATON CUMMINGS . . *Associate Professor.*
[2]GRACE EMILY COOLEY *Instructor.*
MAUDE GILCHRIST . . *Instructor.*
MARGARET CLAY FERGUSON *Instructor.*
HARRIET ANN WALKER . *Assistant in Laboratories.*

Department of Chemistry.

[2]CHARLOTTE FITCH ROBERTS, B.A., Wellesley . . . *Associate Professor.*
CHARLOTTE ALMIRA BRAGG, B.S., Mass. Institute Technology, *Associate Professor.*
EDA MAY CLARK, B.L., Michigan University . . *Instructor.*
MAY BANTA, B.S., Wellesley . . . *Instructor.*
MARY MARION FULLER . . *Assistant in Chemical Laboratories.*
HENRY PAUL TALBOT, S.B., Ph.D. *Nonresident Lecturer on Qualitative and Quantitative Analysis.*

Department of Physics.

SARAH FRANCES WHITING . . *Professor of Physics and Physical Astronomy*
MABEL AUGUSTA CHASE, M.A., Cornell University *Instructor.*

Department of History.

KATHERINE COMAN, Ph.B., Michigan University . . *Professor of History and Economics.*
MARY ALICE KNOX, B.A., Elmira College . . *Associate Professor.*
ELIZABETH KIMBALL KENDALL, LL.B., Boston University *Associate Professor.*
CAROLINE MILES, Ph.D., Ann Arbor . . . *Instructor.*

[2] Absent.

Department of Philosophy.

[a]ANNE EUGENIA MORGAN, M.A., Oberlin . . . . *Professor.*
MARY SOPHIA CASE, B.A., Michigan University . *Associate Professor of Psychology and History of Philosophy.*
MARY WHITON CALKINS, M.A., Smith College . *Instructor.*
ELIZA RITCHIE, B.L., Dalhousie University
M.A., Cornell University . *Instructor.*

Department of History of Art.

ELIZABETH HARRIET DENIO . . . . . . *Professor.*
ETHEL PATON, B.A., Wellesley College . . . . *Instructor.*

Department of Geology.

WILLIAM HARMON MILES, M.A., Wesleyan University
Ph.B., Yale College . . . *Professor.*
CAROLINE EMMA CROSS, Honours Degree, Cambridge, Eng. . *Instructor in Mineralogy.*

Department of Zoölogy.

MARY ALICE WILLCOX . . . . *Professor.*
CAROLINE AUGUSTA WOODMAN, B.S., Mass. Inst. of Tech.
M.A., Vassar . . . *Instructor in Physiology.*
ALBERT PITTS MORSE . . . . *Instructor in Zoölogical Laboratories.*

Department of Mathematics.

ELLEN A. HAYES, B.A., Oberlin . . . . . *Professor.*
EVA CHANDLER, B.A., Michigan University . . *Associate Professor.*
ELLEN LOUISE BURRELL, B.A., Wellesley College . *Associate Professor.*
ELLEN FITZ PENDLETON, M.A., Wellesley College . *Instructor.*
HELEN A. MERRILL, B.A., Wellesley College . . *Instructor.*

Department of English Literature.

KATHARINE LEE BATES, M.A., Wellesley College *Professor.*
[b]VIDA DUTTON SCUDDER, M.A., Smith College . *Associate Professor.*
SOPHIE JEWETT . . . . *Instructor.*
MARGARET POLLOCK SHERWOOD, B.A., Vassar College . *Instructor.*
ISABEL EVANGELINE GRAVES, Ph.B., Wesleyan University *Instructor.*

[a] Abroad on Sabbatical Year.
[b] Absent.

Department of Rhetoric and English Language.

MARGARET ELIZABETH STRATTON, M.A., Oberlin	*Professor.*
SARAH COZZENS WEAVER	*Instructor.*
ELLA GOODENOW WILLCOX	*Instructor.*
SOPHIE CHANTAL HART	*Instructor.*
GEORGE PIERCE BAKER	*Nonresident Lecturer on Argumentative Composition.*

Department of Hebrew and Old Testament History.

SARA ANNA EMERSON, B.A., Boston University	*Associate Professor.*
LUCIA FIDELIA CLARK	*Instructor.*

Department of Elocution.

MARY ADAMS CURRIER	*Professor.*
CORA ELIZABETH EVERETT	*Instructor.*

Bible Study.

OLD TESTAMENT.

SARA ANNA EMERSON, M.A., Boston University	*Instructor.*
LUCIA FIDELIA CLARK	*Instructor.*

NEW TESTAMENT.

SARAH FRANCES WHITING	*Instructor*
ANNE EUGENIA MORGAN, M.A., Oberlin	*Instructor.*
ANGIE CLARA CHAPIN	*Instructor.*
MARY ALICE KNOX, B.A., Elmira College	*Instructor.*
MARY S. CASE, B.A., Michigan University	*Instructor.*
VIDA D. SCUDDER, M.A., Smith College	*Instructor.*
LOUISE ALLEN KELLOGG	*Instructor.*

School of Music.

Junius Welch Hill	Professor of Music and Director of School of Music.
Frank Eugene Morse	Teacher of Vocal Culture.
Emily Josephine Hurd	Teacher of Piano.
George William Bemis	Teacher of Guitar.
Estelle Taylor Andrews	Teacher of Piano.
Marietta Sherman Raymond	Teacher of Violin.
Isabelle Moore Kimball	Teacher of Piano.
Emma Susan Howe	Teacher of Vocal Culture.
Willia Thomas Stovall	Organist and Teacher of Piano and Harmony.
Minnie Adaline Stowell	Teacher of Piano.

School of Art.

Theodore Wendel	Director of School of Art. Instructor in Drawing and Painting.
Agnes Hastings	Instructor in Drawing from Antique and Water Color Painting.

Officers.

Harriet Hawes	Librarian Emeritus
Lydia Boker Godfrey, Ph.B., Boston University	Librarian and Instructor in Bibliography.
Carrie Frances Pierce, B.A., Wellesley	Reference Librarian.
Rachel Taylor Speakman, M.D., Woman's Medical College, Philadelphia, and Cleveland Homœopathic College.	Resident Physician.

EMILIE JONES BARKER, M.D., New York Medical College and
    Hospital for Women . . . . *Resident Physician and Superintendent of Eliot.*
LUCILE EATON HILL. *Director of Gymnasium.*
MARY ANNA WOOD *Physical Examiner, Department of Physical Culture.*
HARTVIG NISSEN . . . . . *Instructor in Swedish Gymnastics.*
SARAH WOODMAN PAUL, B.A., Wellesley *Secretary of the College.*
MARY CASWELL . . . *Secretary to the President.*
AGNES GOODELL . . . . *Registrar.*
CATHERINE AYER RANSOM . *Cashier.*
ABBY CORA JACKSON . . . *Assistant Cashier.*
CAROLINE BROCKWAY BUTLER . *Superintendent of General Office.*
BERTHA LYDIA CASWELL . *Assistant to the Secretary.*
ANNA STEDMAN NEWMAN *Superintendent of Norumbega Cottage.*
LOUISE ANNE DENNISON . *Superintendent of Freeman Cottage.*
LOVINA BRECKENRIDGE NASH *Superintendent of Wood Cottage.*
FREDONIA WHITING CASE . *Superintendent of Domestic Department, College Hall.*
MARY GRALFE NIAS *Superintendent of Domestic Department, Stone Hall.*
FRANCES LOUISE MORTON *Steward.*
CARRY M. TORREY . *Housekeeper, College Hall.*
FRANCES V. DOANE . *Assistant Superintendent of Eliot.*

Alumnae and Classes.

"We are ancients of the earth,
And in the morning of the times."

Graduate Students.

ADAMS, ALICE D., Wellesley	Auburndale, Mass.
ALLEN, ALICE M., Wellesley	36 Washington Square, Gloucester, Mass
BANCROFT, EDITH, Wellesley	Reading, Mass.
CONANT, MARTHA P., Wellesley	Natick, Mass.
CUSHING, M. GERTRUDE, Wellesley	Hotel Brunswick, Boston, Mass.
DEWEY, EMMA GRACE, Wellesley	Jacksonville, Ill.
EDWARDS, MRS. MAY ALDEN, Wellesley	Essex St., Longwood, Mass.
HAYES, MABEL ANNIE, Wellesley	122 Washington St., Malden, Mass
HALL, AMELIA A., Wellesley	Westerly, R. I.
LANCES, FRANCES, Wellesley	Wilkes-Barre, Penn.
PENNIMAN, SARAH ELLA, Wellesley	188 Broadway, Lawrence, Mass.
WADE, CLARA L., Wellesley	Helena, Montana.
CAROLINE L. WILLIAMSON, Wellesley	

A Declaration of Dependence.

WHEN, in the course of human events, it becomes necessary for a class to dissolve the bonds which have connected them with college life, and to assume, among the powers of the earth, the separate and equal station to which the laws of nature and their own opinion of their learning and importance entitle them, a decent respect to their *Alma Mater* requires that they should declare the grief which moves them at the separation.

Prudence, indeed, would dictate (this have we learned line upon line, precept upon precept, from our foster mother) that conditions long established should not be changed for light and transient causes. But when a long train of courses and matriculations, pursuing invariably the same object, has fulfilled its design of reducing us under an absolute sense of our profound ignorance, there is its beneficent task ended, and it is our right, our duty to throw off such conditions and to provide new fields for our future activity. The history of the present Faculty in its relations with the Class of '94, is a history of continued kindness and of repeated benefits (sometimes, we confess, these blessings were so disguised that we failed to recognize them), having in direct object that knowledge of folly which is wisdom, and that mild and submissive disposition which is the crown of womanly character. To prove this let facts be submitted to a candid world.

They have maintained, often against our will, laws the most wholesome, and the most necessary for the public good.

In every stage of our history we have petitioned in humble terms for that which seemed necessary and convenient for us; our repeated petitions have been answered by repeated refusals. Thus has an overruling wisdom preserved us from error.

We, therefore, the representatives of the Class of '94, do, in the name of the class, solemnly publish and declare that this Class of '94 is not, and never can be, unmindful of these benefits; that nothing can absolve them from their allegiance to their *Alma Mater*; and that the affectionate connection between them and Wellesley College cannot now, or at any other time, be totally dissolved.

EMPIRICAL EGOS.

Adelaide M. Abell   Mary C. Adams.   Grace C. Albee.   Rosa N. Allen.   Marion W. Anderson.

L. Gertrude Angell.   Lucy C. Barkwill.   Elizabeth Bartholomew.   Eliza A. Bateman.   Clarissa Benson.

Sarah H. Bixby.   Isabella Black.   Harriet M. Blake.   Anna H. Blauvelt.   Adeline L. Bonney.

Mary Louise Boswell.   Mary Bowles.   Ruby P. Bridgman.   F. Christine Brooks.   Lucy P. Brownell.

EMPIRICAL EGOS — Continued.

Julia S. Burlington.	S. Julia Burgess.	Sarah Burrowes.	Isabella Campbell.	Marion Canfield.
Grace Carr.	Eleanor S. Chase.	Catharine R. Collins.	Mary K. Conyngton.	Louise Cook.
Grace I. Coombs.	Virginia Corbin.	Elva C. Coulter.	Edith R. Crapo.	Florence W. Davis.
Mabel C. Dodge.	Helen P. Drake.	Susie W. Eaton.	Grace O. Edwards.	Caroline W. Field.

EMPIRICAL EGOS -- Continue

Annette Finnigan.   Helen Foss.   Harriet A. Friday.   Cleoma Glass.   Fannie B. Greene.

Elisabeth B. Hardee.   Susan S. Hawley.   Mary Herrick.   Helen Ruth Hibbard.

Alma Hippen.   Mary H. Holmes.   Mary K. Isham.   Bertha C. Jackson.   Edith Judson.

Blanche E. C. Staples.   Alice W. Kellogg.   Eleanor N. Kellogg.   Clara Kruse.   Abigail H. Laughlin.

EMPIRICAL EGOS — Continue

Mabel W. Learoyd.   Bertha E. Longley.   Grace R. McFarland.   Elizabeth M. McGuire.   Effie MacMillan.

Helen MacMillan.   Mary W. Marvell.   Laura I. Mattoon.   Mary Millard.   Marion Mitchell.

Jeannette A. Moulton   Clara Nichols.   Stella M. Osgood.   Carrie J. Peck.   Millicent L. Peirce.

Grace H. Perkins.   Anna K. Peterson.   Louise J. Pope.   Grace I. Porter.   Edna F. Pressey.

EMPIRICAL EGOS - Continued.

Lillian Quinby. Caroline F. Randolph. Mary Russell. Mary J. Salter. Evangeline L. Sherwood

Emily Shultz. A. Theodora Skidmore. Delia Smith. Levenia D. Smith. Mary Ellen Smith.

Helen R. Stahr. Clara Stanwood. Ethel Stanwood. Annie L. Vinal. Roxana H. Vivian.

M. Louise Wetherbee. Martha C. Wilcox. Jane Williams. Elizabeth M. Wood. Alice I. Wood.

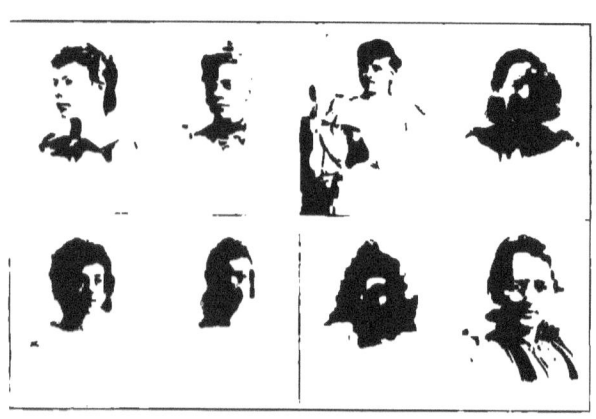

EMPIRICAL EGOS - Continued.

Sarah D. Wyckoff.   Edith E. Tuxbury.   Bessie C. Tuttle.   Mary C. Tracy.

Ellen D. Townshend.   Florence M. Tobey.   Blanche L. Thayer.   Artemesia Stone.

THE TRANSCENDENTAL EGO.

Tree .... Willow.
Flower ... Nasturtium.

Colors ... Green and Silver
Motto ... Doe ye nexte thynge.

Class of Ninety-Four.

YELL.
Rah, Rah, Rah! Rah, we roar;
Wellesley! Wellesley! '94.

Officers.

L. GERTRUDE ANGELL, Z A	President.
HELEN FOSS, Φ Σ	Vice President.
RUBY P. BRIDGMAN, T Z E	Recording Secretary.
FANNIE BRADLEY GREENE, S. S.	Corresponding Secretary.
ISABELLE CAMPBELL	Treasurer.
MARY KENT ISHAM, Z A	First Historian.
MARY LOUISE BOSWELL, Z A	Second Historian.
HARRIET ALICE FRIDAY, T Z E	First Factotum.
MABEL W. LEAROYD, Agora	Second Factotum.
A. THEODORA SKIDMORE	⎫
ROXANA H. VIVIAN	⎬ Executive Committee.
ELEANOR N. KELLOGG, Agora	⎭

Members.

ABELL, ADELAIDE MAE	19 Farrington Avenue, Allston, Mass.
ADAMS, MARIE COOPER	309 College Avenue, Davenport, Iowa.
ALDER, GRACE C., C. S.	42 Chestnut Street, Melrose, Mass.
ALLEN, ROSA NOYES	Bean's Corner, Franklin County, Maine.
ANDERSON, MARION WHARTON, S. S.	Wellesley, Mass.
ANGELL, L. GERTRUDE, Z A	506 Bouck Avenue, Buffalo, N. Y.
BARKWELL, LUCY C.	202 Sawtelle Avenue, Cleveland, Ohio.
BARTHOLOMEW, ELIZABETH, S. S.	Jeansville, Pa.

BATEMAN, ELIZA A., Agora . . Still River, Mass.
BENSON, S. CLARISSA. Agora . College Park, Gambier, Ohio.
BIXBY, SARAH HATHAWAY, Agora 138 North Hill Street, Los Angeles, Cal.
BLACK, ISABELLA, C. S. . . . 23 Tremont Street, Taunton, Mass.
BLAKE, HARRIET MANNING, S. S. . 715 Corinthian Avenue, Philadelphia, Pa.
BLAUVELT, ANNA HUTTON. Z A Roselle, New Jersey
BONNEY, ADELINE LOIS, S. S. . 208 High Street, Portland, Maine.
BOSWELL, MARY LOUISE, Z A . Avondale, Cincinnati, Ohio.
BOWLES, MARY E. . . . . . 1105 Broadway, Kansas City, Mo.
BRIDGMAN, RUBY PORTER, T Z E . 71 Maple Street, Hyde Park, Mass.
BROOKS, FANNIE CHRISTINE, T Z E 348 Franklin Avenue, Cleveland, Ohio.
BROWNELL, LUCY PEARCE, Agora . 42 Thames Street, Newport, R. I.
BUFFINGTON, JULIA STEVENS, Z A . Swansea, Mass.
BURGESS, SARAH JULIA, Agora . Silon Creek, N. Y.
BURROWES, SARAH, Φ Σ . . . Keyport, N. J.
CAMPBELL, ISABELLE . . . 1711 N. Street, Washington, D. C.
CANFIELD, MARION, Z A . . Burlington, Vermont.
CARR, GRACE BARRELLE . 39 West Emerson Street, Melrose, Mass.
CHACE, ELEANOR S. . . . . 20 Dutfee Street, Fall River, Mass.
COLLINS, CATHERINE ROSS, Z A 1559 Garrard Avenue, Covington, Ky.
CONYNGTON, MARY K., Z A . Fort Worth, Texas.
COOK, LOUISE . . . . . 530 Hancock Street, Brooklyn, N. Y.
COOMBS, GRACE IRVING . . Charles River Village, Mass.
CORBIN, VIRGINIA J. . . East McDonaugh, N. Y.
COULTER, ELVA C. . . 2 Plymouth Street, Back Bay District, Boston, Mass.
CRAPO, EDITH RAY, S. S. . . . 513 North 6th Street, Burlington, Iowa.
DAVIS, FLORENCE WADLEIGH, C. S. 1 Grace Avenue, Dorchester, Mass.
DODGE, MABEL CLARA . . . 55 Linden Street, Montclair, N. J.
DRAKE, HELEN PARKER, Z A . . 517 Pine Street, Manchester, N. H.
EATON, SUSIE W, ... Danvers, Mass.
EDWARDS, GRACE OSBORNE, T Z E 1304 Cass Street, La Crosse, Wis.
FIELD, CAROLINE W., Agora . Belfast, Me.
FINNIGAN, ANNETTE, T Z E . . 90 Gold Street, New York, N. Y.
FOSS, HELEN, Φ Σ . . . . 2043 Arch Street, Philadelphia, Pa.
FRIDAY, HARRIET ALICE, T Z E . 316 Fourth Street, Warren, Pa.
GLASS, CLEONA M. A. . . . . 9 Noxon Street, Poughkeepsie, N. Y.
GREENE, FANNIE BRADLEY, S. S. . Auburndale, Mass.
HARDEE, ELISABETH BAILEY, S. S. 76 Gevinett Street, Savannah, Ga.
HAWLEY, SUSAN S., Agora . 25 Myrtle Street, Manchester, N. H.

HERRICK, MARY A. . . . . . Boxford, Mass.
HIBBARD, HELEN RUTH, Agora 29 Church Street, Gloucester, Mass.
HIPPEN, ALMA H., T Z E . 331 South Fourth Street, Pekin, Ill.
HOLMES, MARY HERBERT Φ Σ . . 165 Sandwich Street, Plymouth, Mass.
ISHAM, MARY KEYT, Z A . . . Oak Avenue, Walnut Hills, Cincinnati, O.
JACKSON, BERTHA CHRISTINE, Agora . Westborough, Mass.
JUDSON, EDITH, Φ Σ . . . . 161 Orange Road, Montclair, N. J.
KELLOGG, ALICE WELCH, Z A . Oakham, Mass.
KELLOGG, ELEANORE, Agora . . Kenwood, N. Y.
KRUSE, CLARA M., Z A . . . Central City, Colo.
LAUGHLIN, ABIGAIL HILL, Agora . 145 High Street, Portland, Me.
LEAROYD, MABEL W., Agora . . Danvers, Mass.
LONGLEY, BERTHA E., Φ Σ . . 19 Crown Street, Worcester, Mass.
McFARLAND, GRACE R. . . . Cambridge, N. Y.
McGUIRE, ELIZABETH M. . . 36 Harvard Street, Rochester, N. Y.
McMILLAN, EFFIE, T Z E . 70 Washington Street, Allegheny, Pa.
McMILLAN, HELEN, T Z E . 70 Washington Street, Allegheny, Pa.
MARVELL, MARY W. . . . 25 Highland Avenue, Fall River, Mass.
MATTOON, LAURA ISABELLA . Springfield, Mass.
MILLARD, MARY, Z A . . 64 First Street, Albany, N. Y.
MITCHELL, MARION S., Φ Σ . Newburg, N. Y.
MOULTON, JENNETTE A., C S . Exeter, N. H.
NICHOLES, S. GRACE . . 318 Chestnut Street, Englewood, Ill.
OSGOOD, STELLA M., Agora . Pittsfield, N. H.
PECK, CAROLYN J., C. S. . Wellesley Hills, Mass.
PEIRCE, MILLICENT L., S. S. . 1 Elms Street, North Adams, Mass.
PERKINS, GRACE H., C. S. . Exeter, N. H.
PETERSON, ANNA K., Agora . McGregor, Ia.
POPE, LOUISE J., S. S. . . Rocky Brook, R. I.
PORTER, GRACE I. . . . 1071 Main Street, Bridgeport, Conn.
PRESSEY, EDNA FRANCES, T Z E 20 Oxford Street, Rochester, N. Y.
QUIMBY, LILLIAN BAKER, C. S. . Westbrook, Me.
RANDOLPH, CAROLINE FITZ, S. S. . 741 East Front St., Plainfield, N. J.
RUSSEL, MARY R. . . . Wellesley, Mass.
SALTER, MARY J., Z A . Duluth, Minn.
SHERWOOD, EVANGELINE L. 530 West Monroe Street, Chicago, Ill.
SHULTZ, EMILY BUDD, Φ Σ . 826 Hudson Street, Hoboken, N. J.
SKIDMORE, ANNA THEODORA . Brookfield Centre, Conn.
SMITH, DELIA . . . . Boone, Ia.
SMITH, LEVENIA DUGAN, S. S. Portsmouth, Ohio.

SMITH, MARY ELLEN . . . Waterbury Centre, Vt.
STAHR, HELEN RUSSEL, S. S. 437 West James Street, Lancaster, Pa.
STANWOOD, CLARA . Wellesley Hills, Mass.
STANWOOD, ETHEL, Φ Σ 76 High Street, Brookline, Mass.
STONE, ARTEMISIA . . 353 West Monument Avenue, Dayton, Ohio.
THAYER, BLANCHE L., C. S. Warsaw, N. Y.
TOBEY, FLORENCE M., Agora . 136 Blue Hill Avenue, Boston, Mass.
TOWNSHEND, ELLEN D. . 286 Dixwell Avenue, New Haven, Conn.
TRACY, MARY CLEMMER . . . Putnam, Conn.
TUTTLE, ELIZABETH C. . . . Corning, N. Y.
TUXBURY, EDITH E. . . . North Tonawanda, N. Y.
VINAL, ANNIE L., Agora . . Westborough, Mass.
VIVIAN, ROXANA H. . . . . 106 Gordon Avenue, Hyde Park, Mass.
WETHERBEE, MARY LOUISE, Agora Athol, Mass.
WILCOX, MARTHA C. . . . 8 Highland Avenue, Medford, Mass.
WILLIAMS, JANE, T Z E . . . 216 Cedar Street, Corning, N. Y.
WOOD, ALICE IDA PERRY, T Z E . 162 St. John's Place, Brooklyn, N. Y.
WOOD, ELIZABETH MORRIS, Z A . 13 Greenville Street, Somerville, Mass.
WYCKOFF, SARAH DELIA . . Dayton, Ohio.

MISS MARIA RUSSELL RUSSELL
Member '94 Ex Off...

Other Candidates for First Degrees.

HENDERSON, ANNIE MAY, '92 . . 112 Leicester Street, Worcester, Mass.
LEMER, MAY. S. S., '93 . . 213 Front Street, Harrisburg, Pa.
NEWCOMB, MARY D., Φ Σ '91 . 37 Seely Avenue, Chicago, Ill.
PECKHAM, SARAH E., '93 . . Kingston, R. I.
ROGERS, FLORENCE S., '93 . . . Brainard Street, New London, Conn.
SLATER, ORA WINONA LOUISE, Agora, '93 . 911 Sixth Street, N. W., Washington, D. C.

Former Members of Ninety-Four.

ARTER, FRANCES BLANCHE . 39 Sibley Street, Cleveland, Ohio.
ASHLEY, RUTH E. . 347 Munroe Avenue, Rochester, N. Y.
BAKER, MARY JONES Mt. Vernon, Ohio.
BARTLETT, FANNIE K. . 508 Division Street, Rockford, Ill.
BAXTER, HARRIET MARION Highgate, Vt.
BELFIELD, ADA M. . 5738 Washington Avenue, Chicago, Ill.
* BREWSTER, ALICE F. . Georgetown, Mass.
BROOKS, EMMA CHRISTY 4643 Lake Avenue, Chicago, Ill.
CHAPIN, ELLA POLLY . 478 Delaware Avenue, Buffalo, N. Y.
CHILD, MARY AUGUSTA Greenwich, Conn.
COBB, EVELYN AUGUSTA 31 South Street, Pittsfield, Mass.
CONNER, SARA KATHERINE 323 Beeler Street, New Albany, Ind.
CORTHELL, ALICE E. . 37 Bellevue Place, Chicago, Ill.
CULVER, MARY . . 623 Merideth Street, Saginaw, E. Side, Mich.
DICKIE, CECILIA Truro, Nova Scotia.
EDGERLY, HARRIE G 36 Main Street, Rochester, N. H.
FITCH, AGNES . Pekin, Ill.
FOWLER, MINNIE MAY Stony Point, N. Y.
FREEMAN, GRACE . Aurora, Ill.
* HANSON, EDITH ABBY . 6 Eastern Avenue, Woburn, Mass.
HICKENLOOPER, SARAH . 116 Dayton Street, Cincinnati, Ohio.
HICKS, GRACE EDNA . 42 Chestnut Street, Providence, R. I.

* Deceased.

HOLDEN, ALICE A.	Bennington, Vt.
HUNTINGDON, SUSAN D.	206 Broadway, Norwich, Conn.
JACOBUS, AGNES	337 N. Griffin Avenue, Los Angeles, Cal.
KARR, MARY D.	645 Pearl Street, Elizabeth, N. J.
KEITH, ANNA JOSEPHINE	Westborough, Mass.
LEWIS, MARGARET C.	Honeybrook, Pa.
LINES, MARY H.	413 Perry Street, Peoria, Ill.
*LITTLE, MABELLE	Auburn, Maine.
LOUDON, NANNIE K.	Georgetown, Ohio.
MERRIAM, MARY E.	Mrs. Charles A. Gwyn, Auburn, New York.
MILLER, ADELAIDE	626 Greenup Street, Covington, Ky.
MORSE, BESSIE OWENS	282 East 48th Street, Chicago, Ill.
NEUBERGER, THERESA	Chicago, Ill.
NORTHROP, CLARA LOUISE	174 Church Street, Middletown, Conn.
PALMER, CORA MILLICENT	Saratoga, Santa Clara County, Cal.
PARMENTER, ESTHER	Clinton, Iowa.
PHELPS, MABEL AMELIA	Wilbraham, Mass.
PIERCE, ELSIE M.	25 West 127th Street, New York, N. Y.
PERRY, ALICE JENNIE	108 Vernon Street, Worcester, Mass.
PEW, GRACE WINCHESTER	Gloucester, Mass.
PORTER, EMILIE WHEATON	Keene, N. H.
PRENTISS, LUELLA R.	La Crosse, Wis.
PULLEN, FRANCES K.	Paris, Ky.
ROBINSON, ABBIE J.	Westerly, R. I.
ROBY, EDITH B.	Winchendon, Mass.
SAWIN, MARY EMMELINE	Mrs. Frederic Weinschenk, 27 Garfield Street, North Cambridge, Mass.
SHERWIN, NANIE A.	1922 Grand Avenue, Denver, Col.
SIMMONS, MARGARET BRECK	Green End, Newport, R. I.
SMITH, BESSIE SARGENT	2 Mason Building, Liberty Square, Boston, Mass.
SMITH, CHARLOTTE GENEVERA	Mrs. John R. Garside, 112 West 71st Street, New York City.
SMITH, OLIVE ELIZABETH	124 Crown Street, Meriden, Conn.
SMITH, OLIVE CHAPMAN	Mrs. William D. Stover, Chicago, Ill.
STUART, FANNIE ESTELLE	Richmond, Maine.
THOMPSON, MAUD	54 East 69th Street, New York, N. Y.
THORPE, JOSEPHINE E.	Fort Miller, N. Y.
TOOF, RUTH BESSIE	Mrs. Battle M. Brown, Memphis, Tenn.

* Deceased.

VANDERBURG, KATE   411 East 2d Street, Jamestown, N. Y.
WESTON, MARIANA A.   Rock Hall, Arden, North Carolina.
WHEELER, MARY SABRINA   Fort Smith, Ark.
WINSLOW, EDITH MARTHA   Mrs. George Willett, Norwood, Mass.

IN MEMORIAM

✠

ALICE F. BREWSTER
Died August 25, 1894.

✠

EDITH ABBY HANSON
Died March 5, 1894.

✠

MABELLE LITTLE
Died October 14, 1894.

Proposition:

The Class of Ninety-Five is the Best and Brightest Class in College.

A. INTRODUCTION.
   I. Definition of terms.
      a. By Class of '95, we mean that body of students which brought the sunshine of their presence to the College in 1891, and must leave it once more in total darkness by their graduation in 1895.
      b. College—Wellesley.

B. PROOF.
   I. They[1] have been told so.
      [Any member of said class will corroborate this statement.]
   II. They believe it themselves.
       They are continually saying so.[2]
       [See any portion of speech made by '95's speaker, before the student body, Tree Day, 1893.]
   III. They surpass other classes.
        a. Physically, for
           Their athletic attainments are fitly symbolized by their class boat, which is five feet longer than any of its predecessors.
        b. Mentally, since
           Junior History has no terrors for them, and no fault could be found in their Midyear examination papers in this subject.
        c. Morally, as is shown by the fact that
           They have been admitted to Senior privileges in Junior year.

[1] Never refer to your subject in this indefinite way.
[2] Is this proof?

C. REFUTATION.

It has been objected that the Class of '95 are weak.
- a. Physically, because they cannot break a champagne bottle without strenuous, and apparently fatiguing exertion. But this objection does not hold, for
  - a1. They did break the bottle finally.
- b. Mentally, especially in botanical science, being unable to distinguish a maple from a sycamore. But this objection has little weight, for
  - b1. All mankind is liable to err, and Nature herself takes centuries for her processes of natural selection.
- c. Morally, because there are traces of conceit in their characters. But this cannot be true, for
  - c1. They deny it themselves.

D. CONCLUSION.

From all this it appears that the Class of '95 is in all respects, and without any possibility of doubt, the best and brightest class in Wellesley College.[1]

Tree . . . Sycamore! Maple! Sycamore - Maple! Colors . . . Lavender and White.
Flower . . Sweet Pea. Motto . . . . Ich Dien.

Class of Ninety-Five.

YELL.
Wah, Hoo, Wah; Wah, Hoo, Wah;
'95, '95, Hah, Hah, Hah.

Officers.

HELEN M. KELSEY, S. S. . . . *President.*
GRACE D. SWEETSER . . . *Vice President.*
CLARA LOUISE WARREN, Φ Σ . . *Recording Secretary.*
MARY EMILY FIELD, Z A . . . *Corresponding Secretary.*
EDITH LA RUE JONES, Z A . . . *Treasurer.*
SARAH C. WEED, Agora . . . *First Historian.*
MARTHA T. WATERMAN, Agora . *Second Historian.*
HELEN N. BLAKESLEE, Z A . . *First Factotum.*
SYBIL V. BOYNTON . . . *Second Factotum.*
MARY GRACE CALDWELL, Agora .
GERTRUDE JONES . . . } *Executive Committee.*
MAY BELLE WILLIS . . }

Members.

ADAMS, MARY COLEMAN . . 586 Columbus Ave., Boston, Mass.
ADDEMAN, GRACE LOUISE, Z A 29 Barnes Street, Providence R. I.
ARTER, FRANCES BLANCHE, T Z E 39 Sibley Street, Cleveland, Ohio.
AUGSBURY, WINIFRED, Z A . 264 Second Avenue, Cedar Rapids, Iowa.
AUSTIN, FANNIE ESTELLE, T Z E . Cooperstown, N. Y.
AUTEN, LYDIA CHAPMAN . Princeville, Ill.
BARKER, SARAH GERTRUDE . Plattsburgh, N. Y.

BARNEFIELD, FLORENCE MAY .	45 Summit Street, Pawtucket, R. I.
BENSON, CLARA MANTER, Agora .	East Carver, Mass.
BISHEE, HELEN MABEL, Agora	Freeport, Maine.
BLAKESLEE, HELEN NOYES, Z A	Mason Terrace, Brookline, Mass.
BOARDMAN, EDITH SEVER .	119 Bagley Street, Central Falls, R. I.
BOYNTON, MYRA LOUISA . .	640 Haverhill Street, Lawrence, Mass.
BOYNTON, SYBIL VERONA .	Woodstock, Vt.
BRANDT, LILLIAN EMILY, Φ Σ	St. Louis, Mo.
BRIGGS, JENNY SHERMAN .	12 Brook Street, Pawtucket, R. I.
BROOKS, EMMA CHRISTY, S. S.	4643 Lake Avenue, Chicago, Ill.
BROOKS, IDA MAY, C. S .	Baldwinville, Mass.
BROOKS, JOSEPHINE D. .	14 Mt. Vernon Street, Fitchburg, Mass.
BROWN, ELIZABETH G. . .	15 Craigie Street, Cambridge, Mass.
CALDWELL, MARY GRACE, Agora	Penacook, N. H.
CANNON, MARY GALPIN, Φ Σ	40 Dwight Place, New Haven, Conn.
CAPPS, SARAH ELLEN, S. S.	Jacksonville, Ill.
CARTER, GERTRUDE, Φ Σ .	61 Church Street, Montclair, N. J.
CARYL, CHRISTINE, S. S.	5756 Rosalie Court, Chicago, Ill.
CHAPIN, MARY ELLE, C. S.	Saxton's River, Vt.
CHASE, MARY ESTER, Φ Σ .	516 Woodland Terrace, Philadelphia, Pa.
CHILD, MARY AUGUSTA . .	Greenwich, Conn.
CHUTE, ANNIE GERTRUDE, C. S	Dedham, Mass.
COALE, MARGARET B. .	Mount Holly, N. J.
COE, SOPHRONIA ISABELLA .	Torrington, Conn.
CONNER, SARA KATHARINE, S. S. .	323 Beeler Street, New Albany, Ind.
CURTIS, LILLIAN FAY . . .	North Weymouth, Mass
DAVISON, MABEL ESTELLE, Φ Σ .	Rockville Centre, Long Island, N. Y.
DENISON, EVA MATTOCKS .	Newton Highlands, Mass.
DENISON, GRACE MARY .	Newtonville, Mass.
DENNIS HELEN, Z A .	30 Central Avenue, Newark, N. J.
DEXTER, EDITH DELANO .	148 Summer Street, New Bedford, Mass.
DICKIE, CECILIA, Agora . .	Truro, N. S.
FACKENTHAL, KATHARINE, Agora .	38 South Fourth Street, Easton, Pa.
FAXON, MARY GANNETT . .	Spencer, Mass.
FIELD, MARY EMILY, Z A .	89 Carleton Street, Portland, Me.
FORBES, FLORENCE THERESE, Z A .	5888 Cabanne Place, St. Louis, Mo.
GODDARD, SUSIE ELLA . . .	Orange, Mass.
GOODRICH, CHARLOTTE, T Z E	Stockbridge, Mass.
HASBROUK, ADAH MAY, Z A .	The Washington, Kansas City, Mo.
HASELTINE, ANNIE MABEL .	West Main and Stout Streets, Portland, Ore.

HEILIG, LUCY BELLE	Catasauqua, Pa.
HILDRETH, FRANCES E.	Auburndale, Mass
HILL, WINIFRED E.	329 Park Avenue, Worcester, Mass.
HOWE, ALICE CLARA	50 Lake Street, Nashua, N. H.
HUNT, ALICE WINDSOR, S. S.	8 Jenckes Street, Providence, R. I.
HUNTINGTON, CORNELIA S., Z A	Milton, Mass.
JACOBUS, CAROLINE W., Φ Σ	Auburndale, Mass.
JAMES, HELEN Φ Σ	West Chester, Pa.
JARVIS, GRACE ELIZABETH	120 W. Grand Street, Elizabeth, N. J.
JONES, EDITH LA RUE, Z A	125 W. Penn Street, Germantown, Pa.
JONES, GERTRUDE	18 Park Street, Newark, N. J.
JONES, MARY LILLIAN, Agora	West Chester, Pa.
KELSEY, HELEN MARIAN, S. S	Theresa, N. Y.
KRECKER, ADA MAY	Fredericksburg, Pa.
KRUM, FLORA	5548 Chamberlain Avenue, St. Louis, Mo
LANCE, HATTIE R.	93 Dana Street, Wilkes-Barre, Pa.
LANCE, MARIAN ENO	93 Dana Street, Wilkes-Barre, Pa.
LEATHERBEE, FLORENCE K.	85 Westland Avenue, Boston, Mass.
LEDYARD, ALETHEA, Z A	Steubenville, Ohio.
LEES, MABEL WINIFRED	Wellesley Hills, Mass.
LEONARD, ANNIE MARIA, C. S	160 Oak Street, Taunton, Mass.
LINES, MARY H.	413 Perry Street, Peoria, Ill.
LITTLE, MARY COLLETTE	128 E. Main Street, Norwalk, Ohio
MARCH, BERTHA	39 South Street, Boston, Mass.
MERRILL, MAY, S. S.	Woodstock, Vt.
MILLER, GRACE, S. S.	Akron, Ohio.
MITCHELL, BESSIE CAMPBELL	220 Granite Street, Manchester, N. H.
MORRILL, BERTHA LURENE	34 Chestnut Street, Chelsea, Mass.
NELSON, KATE WINTHROP, Z A	Calais, Me.
NICHOLS, CLARA LOUISE	112 Main Street, Woburn, Mass.
NORCROSS, ALICE WHITNEY, T Z E	16 Claremont Street, Worcester, Mass.
NOURSE, HARRIET ALMIRA	8 Church Street, Marlboro, Mass.
PEALE, ELIZABETH HALE, Z A	262 Fairview Street, Lock Haven, Pa.
PHINNEY, EMMA HENRIETTA	517 W. Market Street, Akron, Ohio.
PITKIN, LILLIE MAY, Φ Σ	Oak Park, Ill.
PRIOR, MARY DAVIS, Agora	13 Plympton Street, Woburn, Mass.
RANDALL, ADELIA MINER	930 Henry Street, Alton, Ill.
ROBERTS, MARY LOUISE	Titusville, Crawford Co., Pa.
ROGERS, ETHEL WARD	84 Gardner Street, Allston, Mass.
SHIRLEY, FLORENCE SOPHIA	Shirley Hill, Manchester, N. H.

SIMMONS, MARGARET BRECK, C. S. Green End, Newport, R. I.
SKELTON, IZA BERNICE . . . 296 Sixth Avenue, Brooklyn, N. Y.
SMITH, ARLINE HAPGOOD, Agora . Athol Highlands, Mass.
SMITH, BESSIE SARGEANT . 2 Mason Building, Liberty Sq., Boston, Mass.
SMITH, EDNA GARDENIER Woodbourne, Sullivan Co., N. Y.
SMITH, LILIAN RICE 512 N. Church Street, Rockford, Ill.
SMITH, MABEL . . . . 40 Mt. Vernon Street, Charlestown, Mass.
STARK, ELIZABETH ALLISON, Φ Σ . 38 Linnaean Street, Cambridge, Mass.
STEPANEK, BEATRICE, C. S. . Walford, Iowa.
STEPHENSON, MARY ELEANOR 300 Stuyvesant Avenue, Brooklyn, N. Y.
STIMPSON, NELLIE JOSEPHINE 19 Sever Street, Worcester, Mass.
STOVER, MARIAN PAULINE Bucksport, Me.
SWEETSER, GRACE DELIA Reading, Mass.
SYKES, MARION . . 782 Warren Avenue, Chicago, Ill.
TAYLER, LOUISE . 20 Scott Street, Youngstown, Ohio.
TAYLOR, MARION LEE 262 Clinton Avenue, Albany, N. Y.
THORPE, JOSEPHINE E. Fort Miller, N. Y.
TODD, ALICE LOVEJOY Calais, Me.
VOORHEES, SOPHIA . Baldwinsville, Onondago, Co., N. Y.
WAITE, ELIZABETH R 125 Stanwood Street, Dorchester, Mass.
WARREN, CLAIRE LOUISE, Φ Σ 429 N. Main Street, Rockford, Ill.
WATERMAN, MARTHA T., Agora 40 Hart Street, New Britain, Conn.
WATSON, FLORENCE OPAL . . Lawton, Mich.
WAYMOUTH, GRACE CROMWELL, S. S. Harvard Street, Cambridge, Mass.
WEAVER, ETHEL , . Washington, D. C.
WEED, SARAH C., Agora . Northfield Seminary, East Northfield, Mass.
WELCH, ALBERTA MAUDE, T Z E . 447 Lexington Avenue, New York, N. Y.
WELLMAN, MABEL THACHER, S. S Newtonville, Mass.
WELLS, EMMA LESLIE . 10 Loomis Street, Montpelier, Vt.
WHITEHOUSE, SARAH F. . Box 28, Augusta, Me.
WILDER, HELEN LOUISE . 34 Elm Street, Jamaica Plain, Mass.
WILLIS, MAY BELLE . 520 Columbus Avenue, Boston, Mass.
WILSON, MARY GERTRUDE, S. S. Jarrettown, Montgomery Co., Pa.
WOODIN, GRACE , . . Great Barrington, Mass.
YOUNG, ELVA HULBURD, Agora Springfield, Mass.
YOUNG, MARY , . . 144 W. Walnut Street, Titusville, Pa.
YOUNG, MARY S. Wyoming, Ohio.

Lusty Juventus.[1]

PROLOGUE.

For as much as man is naturally prone
To evil from his youth, as Scripture doth recite,
It is necessary that he be speedily withdrawn
From naughtiness and sin, his natural appetite.
Give him no liberty in youth, nor his folly excuse;
Bow down his neck, and keep him in good awe,
Lest he be stubborn: no labour refuse
To train him to wisdom, and teach him the law.

Here entereth LUSTY JUVENTUS, *or Youth, clad in flaunting costume of red and white, and singeth the following:—*

In a herber green, asleep where as I lay,
The birds sang sweet in the middes of the day;
I dreamed fast of mirth and play:
In youth is pleasure, in youth is pleasure.

Enter NAUGHTINESS. *Here followeth in dumb show the temptation of L. J. by* NAUGHTINESS. *L. J. yieldeth for a time, and doth play many mischievous and wicked pranks. His little sister appeareth upon the scene, and he tormenteth her with grievous tortures, 'till she doth run away weeping, and* NAUGHTINESS *clappeth his hands. Then the sister, grown somewhat older, appeareth once more, and* NAUGHTINESS *doth incite the two to a quarrel, in which they pelt each other with missiles till they are weary. During the whole quarrel both parties shall scream most lustily, and* NAUGHTINESS *shall*

---

[1] The author has been accused of plagiarism from an old English morality known as *Lusty Juventus*; but it should be remembered that youth is essentially the same in all lands and ages, and its follies might well inspire the same sentiments in independent writers.

dance in glee. Then entereth to them REPENTANCE, *and taketh L. J. by the hand.* NAUGHTINESS *feigneth death, while L. J. speaketh:—*

    O sinful flesh, thy pleasures are but vain;
      Now I find it true, as my teachers did say,
    Broad and pleasant is the path which leadeth unto pain,
      But unto happiness full narrow is the way.
    I followed mine own lusts, the flesh I did not tame,
    And had them in derision which would not do the same;
    Yet mercy hath to me been granted,
    As well as respite my life to amend.
    From the bottom of my heart I repent my iniquity,
    I will walk in the law unto my life's end,
    And my whole delight shall be to live therein,
    Utterly abhorring all naughtiness and sin.

During this speech NAUGHTINESS *shall slyly make faces at the audience, winking one eye and extending the tongue; and when* REPENTANCE *hath led away L. J. he shall rise and dance right merrily, while L. J. in the distance is heard to say:—*

    Now Naughtiness, that wicked sprite,
    Shall never more our realm affright:
    For that he lieth full dead I know,
    And ne'er again shall cause us woe.

Tree . . . . Tupelo.   Colors . . White and Crimson.
Flower . . . Alban Rose.   Motto . . Be your ain sel'.

Class of Ninety-Six.

YELL.
Rickety, Crix; Rickety, Crix;
Wellesley, Wellesley, '96.

Officers.

JOANNA S. PARKER, Agora.	*President.*
MARTHA H. SHACKFORD, Z A	*Vice President.*
HELEN F. COOKE.	*Recording Secretary.*
JULIA H. LYMAN, Φ Σ.	*Corresponding Secretary.*
CORA E. STODDARD, Agora.	*Treasurer.*
S. VIRGINIA SHERWOOD, S. S.	*First Historian.*
SARAH L. HADLEY, Agora	*Second Historian.*
MARTHA A. BULLIS	*First Factotum.*
AMY F. BOUTELLE	*Second Factotum.*
CARLOTTA M. SWETT, S. S.	
CLARA L. WILLIS, Z A	*Executive Committee.*
CLARA R. KEENE	

Members.

ADAMS, ELIZABETH S., S. S.	Wellesley Hills, Mass.
ALLEN, DORA E., S. S.	Navy Yard, Portsmouth, N. H.
ANDERSON, KATHARINE F.	25 Stiles Street, Elizabeth, N. J.
BAKER, ALBERTA F., Agora	1244 Wrightwood Avenue, Chicago, Ill.
BALDWIN, HARRIET R., Φ Σ	41 Broad Street, Middletown, Conn.
BARTLESON, BLANCHE	1200 Chestnut Avenue, Minneapolis, Minn.
BATCHELDER, JOSEPHINE H.	Holliston, Mass.

BEALE, JENNIE R. . . . . 37 West Second Street, Frederick City, Md.
BEEBE, ALICE G. . . . . Nantucket, Mass.
BELFIELD, ADA M., S. S. . . 5738 Washington Avenue, Chicago, Ill.
BLANCHARD, AUGUSTA H. . . 165 State Street, Portland, Me.
BOARMAN, ALICE L. . . . 451 Magazine, corner Robin Street, New Orleans, La.
BOGARDUS, BELINDA M., Agora . Mt. Vernon, O.
BOUTELLE, AMY F. . . . . 12 Mechanic Street, Fitchburg, Mass.
BROTHWELL, BELLE P. . . . Torrington, Conn.
BROWN, EMILY H., Z A . . . 2 Canal Street, Woburn, Mass.
BULLIS, MARTHA A. . . . 37 Laurens Street, Olean, N. Y.
BURNETT, CHARLOTTE F. . . Price Hill, Cincinnati, O.
BURNS, BESSIE L. . . . . 45 Granite Street, Quincy, Mass.
BUTLER, EDITH E. . . . . 62 Central Avenue, Hyde Park, Mass.
BYERS, JANE A. . . . . . Sycamore, Ill.
CALDWELL, AGNES LOUISE, Z A . Shelbyville, Ky.
CAPRON, MAUDE E. . . . . Smithfield Avenue, Providence, R. I.
CHANDLER, HELEN E. . . . 18 Rockland Street, Taunton, Mass.
CHIPMAN, INA M. . . . . Berwick, Kings Co., Nova Scotia.
CHRISTIE, MARY W. . . . 106 Central Avenue, Chelsea, Mass.
CLARKE, HARRIET B. . . . Dover, Ill.
COALE, MARGARET B. . . . Arch Spring, Blair Co., Pa.
COBB, ANNE E., Agora . . . Newton Centre, Mass.
COLBY, ANNIE W. . . . . 348 Manchester Street, Manchester, N. H.
COOKE, HELEN F., Agora . . North Brookfield, Mass.
CUSHING, ELLEN M. . . . 27 Holt Street, Fitchburg, Mass.
DARTT, MARY A. . . . . Springfield, Vt.
DAVENPORT, MARY F. . . . Mount Auburn, Mass.
DAVIDSON, MARY E. . . . 1630 Washington Avenue, Scranton, Pa.
DAVIS, MARY A. . . . . 241 Oakwood Boulevard, Chicago, Ill.
DE COU, HELENA, Agora . . Plainfield, N. J.
DENNIS, GERTRUDE L. . . . 53 Highland Street, Worcester, Mass.
DUDLEY, HELEN M., Φ Σ . . Riverside, Cincinnati, O.
DUXBURY, JENNIE J., S. S. . . 179 Central Avenue, Dover, N. H.
EGINTON, SARAH L. . . . Winchester, Ky.
EVANS, JESSIE . . . . . 1524 No. 15th Street, Philadelphia, Pa.
FISKE, ISABELLA H. . . . Wellesley Hills, Mass.
FLETCHER, MARTHA ELIZABETH . Pepperell, Mass.
FOSTER, ALICE H. . . . . 99 West Street, Worcester, Mass.
FOSTER, SADIE P. . . . . 268 South Main Street, St. Albans, Vt.

GENUNG, ANNA M. 44 Avon Avenue, Newark, N. J.
GEYER, EMMA L. 330 Wayne Avenue, Dayton, Ohio
GODFREY, GRACE 17 Court Square, Milford, Mass.
HADLEY, SARAH L., Agora South Canterbury, Conn.
HALLAM, FLORENCE M. Centralia, Ill.
HAYNES, ELIZABETH Franklin, Tenn.
HAWKES, MINNIE E. Bardwell's Ferry, Franklin Co., Mass.
HEFFERAN, MARY, Z A 272 Fountain Street, Grand Rapids, Mich.
HENRY, ADA M 342 Bates Avenue, St. Paul, Minn.
HERSHEY, FRANCES G. 609 Avenue B., Sterling, Ill.
HOWARD, ETHEL L. 16 West Street, Worcester, Mass.
HOWLAND, BLANCHE R. 509 Columbus Avenue, Boston, Mass.
HOYT, AMELIA H. 2 Hillside Place, Danbury, Conn.
HOYT, SOPHIA O. Portsmouth, N. H.
HUNTINGTON, THERESA L., Φ Σ Milton, Mass.
HYATT, BERTHA E. 358 Madison Avenue, Albany, N. Y.
INGALLS, HANNAH E. Abington, Conn.
JACOBS, BLANCHE S. Melrose Highlands, Mass.
JANSSEN, CORNELIA M. 2116 Minnie Avenue, Kansas City, Mo.
JOHNSON, BESSIE H. 38 South Bow Street, Milford, Mass.
KAHN, IRENE, C. S 413 North 6th Street, St. Joseph, Mo.
KEENE, CLARA R. Brighton, Mass.
KELLOGG, MAY E., T Z E 55 Pomeroy Avenue, Pittsfield, Mass.
KENDALL, EVANGELINE Dunstable, Mass.
KERR, ANNIE C. 243 Hamilton Avenue, Paterson, N. J.
KING, CAROLINE W., T Z E Willet's Point, Long Island.
KITTINGER, MARGARET M. 530 Porter Avenue, Buffalo, N. Y.
LANCRAFT, IDA M. Fair Haven Heights, New Haven, Conn.
LANE, AMY S. North Hadley, Mass.
LITTLE, MARY E. 510 No. King Street, Xenia, Ohio.
LOUDON, EVA Georgetown, Ohio.
LUNT, MARY R, T Z E 464 West 144th Street, New York City, N. Y.
LYMAN, JULIA H., Φ Σ 200 Ashland Boulevard, Chicago, Ill.
McCHESNEY, ANNA K 821 River Street, Troy, N. Y
McDOWELL, PAULINE 20 Spruce Street, Newark, N. J.
McKINNEY, NELLIE GERTRUDE 143 Henry Street, Binghamton, N. Y.
MARGESSON, HELEN P. 16 Dix Street, Dorchester, Mass.
MATHEWS, ANNA ELIZABETH Billerica, Mass.
MILLARD, MAUDE L. Box 266, Wellesley, Mass
MILLER, GRACE M. Le Roy N. Y.

MONTGOMERY, MARY W., Z A   Adana, Turkey, care Rev. C. W. Park, Derby, Conn.
MOORE, H. ISABELLE   Chestnut Hill, Mass.
MORGAN, GRACE E.   Essex, Conn.
MUDGETT, MARY L., S. S.   Plymouth, N. H.
MUSHALL, ELIZABETH H.   204 High Street, Germantown, Phila., Pa.
MUNROE, M. ADRIENE   43 Warren Street, Woburn, Mass.
NEVERS, CORDELIA C.   St. Johnsbury, Vt
NORTHUP, LAURA H.   261 14th Street, Portland, Ore.
NUTTER, GRACE A.   16 James Street, Bangor, Me.
PARK, CORNELIA. S. S.   Derby, Conn.
PARKER, JOANNA S., Agora   Atchison, Kansas.
PEAKS, ANNIE H., Agora   Dover, Me.
PULLEN, FRANCES K., Φ Σ   Paris, Kentucky.
RAND, MABEL F., C. S.   Whitman, Mass.
RHOADES, EDITH M., Agora   514 North 4th Street, St. Joseph, Mo.
ROBINSON, ANNIE M.   Reading, Mass.
ROTHSCHILD, CONSTANCE L.   4 East 67th Street, New York, N. Y.
ROWE, HETTY M.   56 So. Clinton Street, Poughkeepsie, N. Y.
RYDER, MARIA D.   46 West Ninth Street, New York, N. Y.
SCHOONOVER, ADELAIDE VIRGINIA, Z A   Madison, N. J.
SCHOULER, ALICE H., Φ Σ   Elkton, Md.
SEATON, SARA   1 Glen Park Place, Cleveland, Ohio.
SHACKFORD, MARTHA HALE, Z A   151 Central Avenue, Dover, N. H.
SHANNON, MARY E.   523 West 4th Street, Duluth, Minn.
SHERWOOD, SARAH VIRGINIA, S. S.   66 Courtland Street, Providence, R. I.
SIZER, CLARA A.   1303 Euclid Avenue, Cleveland, Ohio.
SMITH, MARY FRAZER   West Chester, Pa.
SNYDER, ELIZABETH R., S. S.   2613 Price Street, St. Louis, Mo.
STODDARD, CORA FRANCES, Agora   East Brookfield, Mass.
STRAIGHT, BERTA K.
SWEET, ADA W.   West Mansfield, Mass.
SWEET, CARLOTTA M., S. S.   130 Hammond Street, Bangor, Me.
SWEET, SARAH LILIAN   Pittsfield, N. H.
THOMAS, PRUDENCE E.   15 Walpole Street, Roxbury, Mass.
TOWNSEND, GRACE B., C. S.   Wellesley Hills, Mass.
TOWNSEND, MARY L.   Cedar Falls, Iowa.
TUELL, ANNIE K.   Milton, Mass.
VON WETTBERG, CLARA E., Φ Σ   464 Farmington Avenue, Hartford, Conn.
WHITCHER, MARY C.   3 Cleveland Avenue, Woburn, Mass.

WILKINS, LYDIA K., T Z E   218 A Street, S. E. Washington, D. C.
WILLIAMS, MARY L.   Burnside, Conn.
WILLIS, CLARA L., Z A   Palmer, Mass.
WILSON, ANNIE F.   Waterford, Oxford Co., Me.
WOOD, ANGIE P.   Athol Highlands, Mass.
WOODIN, MARY F. Σ   Oneonta, N. Y.
WOODWARD, MARY A.   Thompsonville, Conn.
WRIGHT, LOTTIE E.   410 I Street, N. W. Washington, D. C.
WYLLIE, EDITH E.   18 Chestnut Street, Chelsea, Mass.
YOUNG, LENA H., Agora   44 Dorchester Street, Springfield, Mass.
ZIEGLER, ANNIE E., Agora   1 Ellis Street, Roxbury, Mass.

A Song of Ninety and Seven.

There's no dew left on the daisies and clover,
    There's no rain left in heaven;
I've said my "seven times" over and over,
    Seven times one are seven.

I am old,—so old I can write a letter;
    My birthday lessons are done.
The lambs play always, they know no better;
    They are only one times one.

O library, open your sacred portal,
    Where wisdom and learning dwell.
O faculty, pour out your stores immortal,
    My treasure of thought to swell.

And show me your hall with the secrets in it;
    I will not steal them away.
I am old; you may trust me. Just for a minute!
    I am 90 and 7 to-day.

I wait for my story; the birds cannot sing it,
    Not one, as he sits on the tree.
The bells cannot ring it, but long years, O bring it!
    Such as I wish it to be.

Tree . . . Pine
Flower . . . Daffodil.

Colors . . . Olive Green and Gold.
Motto . . . Let the deed show.

Class of Ninety-Seven.

Officers.

ELIZABETH G. EVANS	*President.*
M. DENISON WILT	*Vice President.*
HELEN M. GORDON	*Recording Secretary.*
CAROLINE M. DAVIS	*Corresponding Secretary.*
LOUISE R. LOOMIS	*Treasurer.*
FLORENCE M. PAINTER	*First Historian.*
BERTHA E. TREHEIN	*Second Historian.*
FLORENCE P. BENNETT	*First Factotum.*
BLANCHE CURRIER	*Second Factotum.*
EDITH A. HOWLAND	
MARY W. MILLER	*Executive Committee.*
GENEVA CRUMB	

Members.

ADAMS, MABEL W.	Wellesley Hills, Mass.
ALBERSON, JESSIE A.	Ashland, Ohio.
ALDEN, CLARA L.	22 Boynton Street, Worcester, Mass.
ALDRICH, AGATHA	Charlton, Mass.
ALLEN, MARY W.	Navy Yard, Portsmouth, N. H.
ATTSHELER, ELIZA	727 Main Street, Louisville, Ky.
ARNOLD, EDNA B.	67 Belmont Street, Pawtucket, R. I.
ATKINS, HELEN L.	Georgetown, Colo.
AULD, FAY	317 N. Fourth Street, Atchison, Kan.
AYERS, RUTH A.	8 N. State Street, Concord, N. H.
BACON, AGNES L.	Abingdon, Ill.
BAUCKER, KATHERINE H.	Jackson, Mich.

BAUCKER, MARTHA W.	305 Wilkins Street, Jackson, Mich.
BARNARD, ANNIE C.	Barnardville, Worcester, Mass.
BARINTZ, SARAH E.	722 Eighteenth Street, Des Moines, Iowa.
BATTISON, MABEL L.	Wollaston, Mass.
BAXTER, EMILY P.	61 Deering Street, Portland, Me.
BEAN, GRACE S.	92 Atlantic Street, Stamford, Conn.
BENNETT, FLORENCE P.	Wrentham, Mass.
BENTLEY, VINNIE B.	1440 North 13th Street, Philadelphia, Pa.
BINGHAM, ANNA M.	West Connvall, Vt.
BIRD, GRACE E.	922 Spruce Street, Philadelphia, Pa.
BIXBY, ANNE L.	138 North Hill Street, Los Angeles, Cal.
BIXBY, BERTHA C.	84 Winthrop Avenue, Revere, Mass.
BLACKBURN, JUDITH A.	1263 Bolton Street, Baltimore, Md.
BLAIR, MILLICENT F.	37 Pinckney Street, East Somerville, Mass.
BLANCHARD, ABBY F.	Brookfield, Mass
BLANCHARD, REBEKAH G.	Bellefonte, Centre Co., Pa.
BOWMAN, MABEL E.	355 Broadway, Somerville, Mass.
BROOKS, MAY	12 Baldwin Street, East Orange, N. J.
BROTHERTON, MARY M.	216 West Adams Street, Los Angeles, Cal.
BROWN, HARRIET H.	Putnam, Conn.
BUETT, GRACE L.	Andover, Mass.
BURCHARD, ALICE W.	5540 Cornell Ave., Chicago, Ill.
BURNHAM, GERTRUDE E.	407 Hanover Street, Manchester, N. H.
CALKINS, EVELYN L.	5053 Madison Avenue, Chicago, Ill.
CARPENTER, FANNIE A.	North Randolph, Vt.
CARTER, HARRIET W.	314 Andover Street, Lawrence, Mass.
CHANDLER, ANNA P.	Needham, Mass.
CHAPMAN, FANNIE L.	345 Spring Street, Portland, Me.
CHEEVER, A. M.	Box 86, North Attleboro, Mass.
CHILDS, ALICE W.	216 Main Street, Amesbury, Mass.
CHIPMAN, INA M.	Berwick, King's Co., Nova Scotia.
COIT, CLARA L.	165 Hudson Street, Rochester, N. Y.
COLLES, JULIA N.	Morristown, N. J.
CORSON, ELLEN P.	31 West Main Street, Norristown, Pa.
COWAN, ALICE B.	65 Powow Street, Amesbury, Mass.
CRAFTS, PHEBE R.	15 West Lorain Street, Oberlin, Ohio.
CRAIG, ELIZA P.	Falmouth, Mass.
CROFUT, FLORENCE S. M.	Danielsonville, Conn.
CROSBY, CORA W.	West Medford, Mass.
CRUMB, GENEVA	Bloomfield, Mo.

CUMMINGS, LULU W. . . Washington, D. C.
CURRIER, BLANCHE . . 65 Temple Street, Haverhill, Mass.
CUSHMAN, ELLEN M. . 20 Mt. Pleasant Street, St. Johnsbury, Vt.
DAMON, ALICE B. . . Box 252 South Framingham, Mass.
DANA, HANNAH L. . . Westbrook, Me.
DAVIS, CAROLINE M. . 12 Mills Street, Somerville, Mass.
DAVIS, JESSIE A. . . 107 North Grant Ave., Crawfordsville, Ind.
DAVIS, MARION T. . . Torrington, Conn.
DENNISON, GRACE M. . 7 Concord Street, Charlestown, Mass.
DEVOL, GERTRUDE . . Gambier, Knox Co., Ohio.
DE WITT, MINNIE E. . Fairport, Monroe Co., N. Y.
DEWSON, MARY W. . . Adams Street, Quincy, Mass.
DIMMICK, ANNIE M. . 435 Clayton Street, Montgomery, Ala.
DISQUE, MARY M. . . 196 Arch Street, Allegheny, Pa.
DODGE, SUSAN W. . . 211 High Street, Newburyport, Mass.
DUDLEY, EDITH . . . 80 School Street, Woonsocket, R. I.
DURFEE, ELIZABETH W. . 637 East Capitol Street, Washington, D. C.
DURRELL, JESSIE M. . 17 Dana Street, Cambridge, Mass.
EDDY, EUGENIA L. . . 38 Highland Avenue, Fitchburg, Mass.
EDGET, GRACE L. . . 329 Cabot Street, Beverly, Mass.
ELY, OLIVE J. . . Corner 40th Street and Greenwood Avenue, Chicago, Ill.
ENNIS, MAUDE . . . Ashaway, R. I.
EVANS, ELIZABETH G. . 570 West Second Street, Dayton, Ohio.
FARBY, ETHEL L. . . Orange, Franklin Co., Mass.
FERGUSON, GERTRUDE . 45 Congress Street, Belfast, Me.
FINNIGAN, BESSIE M. . 90 Gold Street, New York, N. Y.
FISHER, ABBY S. . . Norwood, Mass.
FLINT, BERTHA . . . 8 Chauncy Street, Cambridge, Mass.
FLOWER, DAISY O. . . 24 Rockland St., Roxbury, Boston, Mass.
FLOWER, HELEN M. . . Rapid City, South Dakota.
FOLEY, FLORENCE . . Lincoln, Ill.
FRENCH, BESSIE M. . . 39 Summer Street, Keene, N. H.
FRENCH, MAUD M. . . 64 Decatur Street, Brooklyn, N. Y.
FYOCK, ALICE M. . . 35th Street and Virginia Avenue, Kansas City, Mo.
FYOCK, ROSE . . . 35th Street and Virginia Avenue, Kansas City, Mo.
GALBRAITH, MARY . . 513 Henly Street, Knoxville, Tenn.
GATES, ANNIE C. . . 17 Court Square, Milford, Mass.

GATES, MARY B. . . 17 Court Square, Milford, Mass.
GIDMAN, THUSA . . Preston, Conn.
GOLDTHWAIT, MARY S. Pleasant Street, Marblehead, Mass.
GORDON, HELEN M. . 182 West Brookline Street, Boston, Mass.
GOULD, MYRABEL J. . Greenfield, Mass.
GRAFF, ELFIE . . 505 West Fourth Street, So. Bethlehem, Pa.
GRISWOLD, CARRIE M. St. Johnsbury East, Vt.
GUY, EVA M . . Rosedale, Ohio.
HAINES, LILLIAN F. North Hampton, N. H.
HALL, GERTRUDE M. 59 Lowell Street, Lawrence, Mass.
HALLETT, MARY W. Mansfield, Mass.
HALSEY, BERTHA M. 3 North Church Street, Schenectady, N. Y.
HARVEY, LULU M. . 31 Pearl Street, St Johnsbury, Vt.
HASBROOK, ETHELBERTA. 170 Hawthorne Avenue, Yonkers, N. Y.
HASTINGS, FLORENCE E. . Colorado Springs, Colorado.
HATHAWAY, MIRIAM . . Middleboro, Mass.
HAWLEY, MARY P. . . 40 Newhall Street, Malden, Mass.
HEARN, ROSA C. . . McKenzie, Tenn.
HICKENLOOPER, AMELIA S. Cincinnati, Ohio.
HILLER, RAY R. . Springfield, Ill.
HISCOX, ELIZABETH M. 7 Mt. Pleasant Avenue, Newark, N. Y.
HOLBROOK, ALICE M. . Sutton, Mass.
HOLBROOK, ELIZABETH L. Danversport, Mass.
HOLDER, HELEN Z. . 32 Commercial Street, Lynn, Mass.
HOLMES, KATHERINE S. Cor. Sixth and Mulbury, Terre Haute, Ind.
HOOPES, EMILY . West Chester, Penn.
HOWARD, GRACE G. Eastondale, Mass.
HOWE, LOUISE C. . Norwich, Conn.
HOWLAND, EDITH A. Waverly Avenue, Newton, Mass.
HUME, RUTH P. . Ahmednagar, West India.
HUNT, EVELYN S. . 1 Prospect Street, Bangor, Me.
HUTCHESON, LOUISE 447 N. Street, N. W., Washington, D, C
IRWIN, EDITH C. . 17 Quincy Place, Yonkers, N. Y.
JOHNSON, EMILY S. . 109 Luzerne Avenue, Pittston, Penn.
KELLOGG, FLORENCE Pittsfield, Mass.
KING, ELIZABETH E. Trumansburg, N. Y.
KNIGHT, EMMA F. . 11 Main Street, Marlboro, Mass.
LADD, EDITH H. . 58 Winthrop Street, Springfield, Mass.
LAIRD, GRACE N. . 14 Gardner Street, Worcester, Mass.
LEWIS, HENRIETTA . 503 East Street, Flint, Mich.

Libby, Mary L.	15 Derring Street, Portland, Me.
Lincoln, Maria L.	Oakham, Mass.
Long, Winnie Hale	261 Chestnut Street, Chelsea, Mass.
Loomis, Louise R.	Auburndale, Mass.
McAllister, A. V.	Walton, Del. County, N. Y.
McDuffee, Fannie E.	Box 91, Rochester, N. H.
McKee, Anna Belle	806 Negleg Avenue, Pittsburgh, E. E. Pa.
Mahl, Alice M.	483 Manhattan Avenue, New York, N. Y.
Marden, Mary L.	Auburndale, Mass.
Marple, Marcia T.	Wollaston Heights, Mass.
Marvell, Harriet T.	25 Highland Avenue, Fall River, Mass.
May, Edith	105 State Street, Albany, N. Y.
Meguire, Abby S.	911 Third Street, Louisville, Ky.
Menet, Anna A.	141 W. 104 Street, New York, N. Y.
Miller, Mary	420 S. 15th Street, Philadelphia, Pa.
Mitchell, Eleanor	Bellefonte, Pa.
Montgomery, Roberta H.	20 Bloss Street, Rochester, N. Y.
Moore, Katherine	216 East Main Street, La Porte, Ind.
Morgan, Lillian B.	315 North Michigan Avenue, Saginaw, Mich.
Moroney, Mary J.	209 Broadway, Pawtucket, R. I.
Morrill, Emma A.	Norwood, Mass
Moses, Josephine A.	612 East 7th Street, Jamestown, N. Y.
Munger, Jessie S.	Knoxboro, N. Y.
Munroe, Evelyn A.	229 Ballou Street, Woonsocket, R. I.
North, Mary	Park Street, Montclair, N. J.
Oakes, Margaret E.	Steinway, Long Island, N. Y.
O'Brien, Helen F.	Abington, Mass.
Ordway, Helen F.	61 Fowle Street, Woburn, Mass.
Painter, Florence M.	Sag Harbor, Long Island, N. Y.
Parker, Maud L.	Thorndike, Mass.
Parkhurst, Hattie M.	6 Court Square, Milford, Mass.
Paul, Ruth A.	Stoughton, Norfolk County, Mass.
Peabody, Elizabeth G.	Holland Patent, Oneida County, N. Y.
Peabody, Marion C.	Reading, Mass.
Pennell, Ethel A.	2 Cedar Avenue, Jamaica Plain, Mass.
Perrin, Ina C.	St. Johns, Mich.
Perry, Temple L.	1802 M Street, Washington, D. C.
Pettee, Helen W.	Sharon, Mass.
Pierce, Mary E.	South Britain, Conn.
Pingrey, Cora E.	Delevan, Catt. County, N. Y.

Pinkham, Mary K. . . 64 Nahant Street, Lynn, Mass.
Piper, Warrene R. . 45 Langdon Street, Cambridge, Mass.
Pomeroy, Gertrude A . Wellesley, Mass.
Porter, Katherine M. . Freeport, Ill.
Prescott, Nellie G. . Randolph, Mass.
Price, Ethelyn M. . 1441 Inslee Street, Denver, Col.
Pritchard, Sydna E. . 10 Tremont Street, Brockton, Mass.
Pullin, Charlotte I. . 28 Lemon Street, Newark, N. J.
Purdy, Blanche M. . 327 Exchange Building, Kansas City, Mo.
Purdy, Clara R. . . Ovid, Seneca County, N. Y.
Purington, Margarette D. . Indiana, Pa.
Ranney, Edith E. . . St. Johnsbury, Vt.
Randall, Elizabeth A. . Great Falls, N. H.
Randell, Julia D. . 930 Henry Street, Alton, Ill.
Rapalje, Louise C. . 18 Prospect Terrace, East Orange, N. J.
Raynal, Frida M. . 427 Madison Avenue, Elizabeth, N. J.
Ready, Mae A. . Painesville, Ohio.
Rhodes, Blanche E. . 5037 Lake Avenue, Chicago, Ill.
Ritchie, Emma G. . West Barnet, Vt.
Robbins, Phila Belle . Wellesley, Mass.
Roberts, Mattie G. . 1306 East Capitol Avenue, Springfield, Ill.
Robson, Olive R . Wellesley Hills, Mass.
Rogers, Mary L. . 50 Clyde Street, Pawtucket, R. I.
Rollins, Hannah E. . Box 670, Dover, N. H.
Rushmore, Gertrude . 751 West 7th Street, Plainfield, N. J.
Secombe, Annabell C. . Milford, N. H.
Shedd, Eva C. . . 2 Thompson Street, Poughkeepsie, N. Y.
Sherburne, Alice E. . South Danville, N. H.
Shoemaker, Mary E. . 130 Water Street, Wilkes Barre, Pa.
Shortle, Annie J. . Provincetown, Mass.
Simonds, Mary E. . 14 Willow Place, Yonkers, N. Y.
Smart, Jennie A. . Hillsboro, N. H.
Smith, Emily M. . Tillipally, Jaffna, Ceylon, India.
Smith, Floyd . . The Washington, Kansas City, Mo.
Smith, Helen K. . Portsmouth, N. H.
Smith, Miriam A. . 378 High Street, Newark, N. J.
Spaulding, Mabel F. . Mansfield, Mass.
Spencer, Addie . Stoneham, Mass.
Spring, Florence G. . 25 Mt. Vernon Street, Fitchburg, Mass.
Spring, Lydia G. . 244 Mt. Pleasant Avenue, Newark, N. J.

STEVENS, ALICE V.	Albany, N. Y.
STIX, EDITH	3135 Washington Avenue, St. Louis, Mo.
STOCKWELL, MARIE L.	Hillside Street, Roxbury, Mass.
STONE, MAUDE A.	11 Fulton Avenue, Rochester, N. Y.
TARBOX, BELLE V.	Farmington, Maine.
TATE, MARY E.	Sioux Falls, South Dakota.
TEBBETTS, MARY E.	519 Essex Street, Lynn, Mass.
THYNG, MARY I.	Laconia, N. H.
TOMPKINS, EMERY C.	216 Coliseum Street, New Orleans, La.
TREBEIN, BERTHA E.	Trebeins, Ohio.
TROTTER, MAUDE A.	4 Mills Street, Roxbury, Mass.
TROWBRIDGE, JEANETTE	14 Church Street, Milford, Mass.
TUCKER, CARRIE M.	Hyde Park, Mass.
TUNBURY, LUNA E.	North Tonawanda, N. Y.
WALES, HORTENSE E.	Bridgton, Maine.
WALL, MABEL P.	52 Myrtle Street, Boston, Mass.
WALLIN, CARRIE E.	Gilbertsville, N. Y.
WARD, GERTRUDE P.	41 Park Place, Bloomfield, N. J.
WARFIELD, JENNIE E.	70 Wyman Street, Brockton, Mass.
WASHBURN, ANNIE M.	299 N. Montello Street, Brockton, Mass.
WAXHAM, M. EVELYN	409 Winnebago Street, Rockford, Ill.
WEST, ELLA	Raritan, Somerset County, N. J.
WETMORE, KATHARINE S.	108 S. Fitzhugh Street, Rochester, N. Y.
WETMORE, LOUISE S.	108 S. Fitzhugh Street, Rochester, N. Y.
WHEELER, LUCIA M.	Troy, Ohio.
WHEELOCK, KATHARINE S.	Hughesville, Pa.
WHITMAN, BERTHA M.	109 Walnut Avenue, Roxbury, Mass.
WHITNEY, CELENA M.	South Ashburnham, Mass.
WHITNEY, MARY A.	Still River, Mass.
WILLIS, RUTH C.	Boston, Mass.
WILSON, ABBIE E.	Nahant, Mass.
WILSON, ISABEL	55 Washington Street, Winchester, Mass.
WILSON, JENNY P.	Indiana, Pa.
WILT, MARY D.	Dayton, Ohio.
WOOD, ELEANOR W.	Bellevue Avenue, Upper Montclair, N. J.
WOOD, GERTRUDE P.	Bellevue, Huron County, Ohio.
WOODIN, CLARA F.	Great Barrington, Berkshire Co., Mass.
WORK, EFFIE A.	108 Park Place, Akron, Ohio.
WRIGHT, EDITH E.	34 Beacon Street, Chelsea, Mass.
YEATON, LILLIAN	66 North State Street, Concord, N. H.

"We have but faith; we cannot know,
For knowledge is of things we see."

Club of Ninety-Eight.

Officers.

FRANCES G. HOYT — *Chairman.*
MARTHA S. DALZELL — *Vice Chairman and Historian.*
LOLA E. CHAPMAN — *Secretary and Treasurer.*
ANNIE A. WALDRON
CATHERINE R. BISBEE — *Executive Committee.*

Members.

BISBEE, CATHERINE R. — Hanover, N. H.
CHAPMAN, LOLA E. — Missouri Valley, Iowa.
DALZELL, MARTHA S. — South Egremont, Mass.
HOYT, FRANCES G. — 153 North 16th Street, Portland, Oregon.
LORD, CAROLYN M. — Calais, Maine.
MASON, HELEN V. — Suffield, Conn.
SPINNEY, MAUDE J. — 1427 West 10th Street, Des Moines, Iowa.
WALDRON, ANNIE A. — Bishops Place, New Brunswick, New Jersey.
WHITE, CHARLOTTE H. — Whately, Mass.

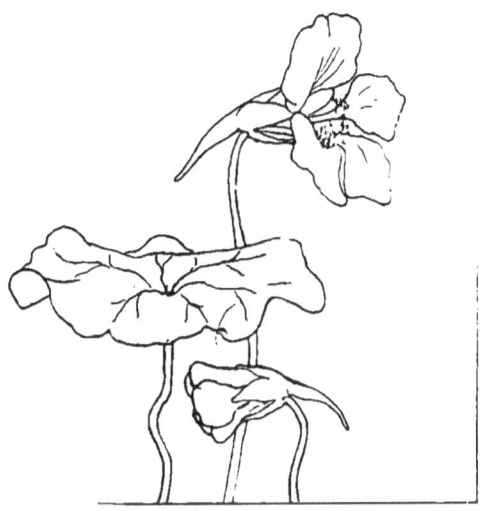

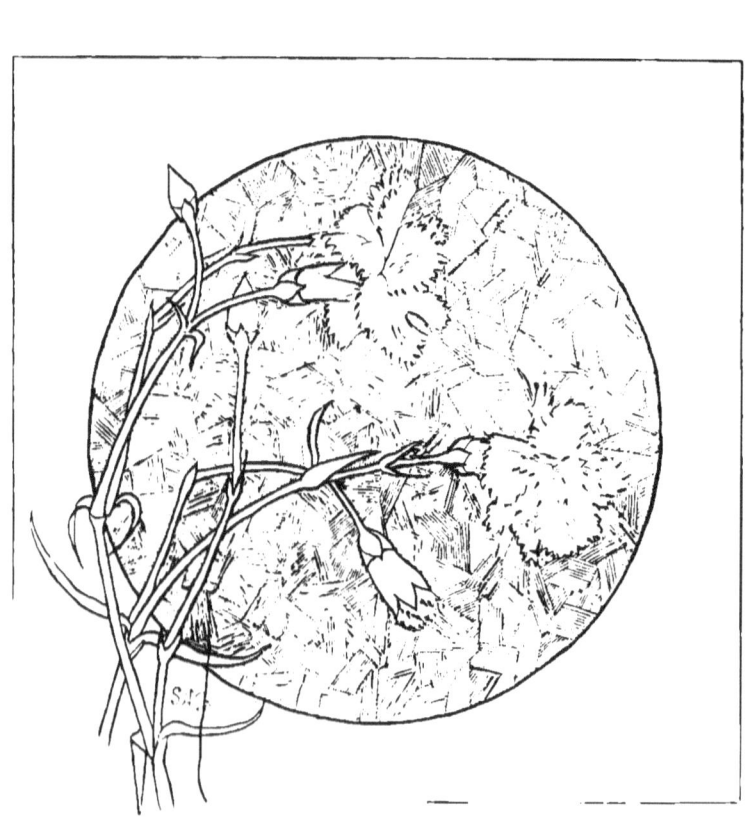

Specially What?

Flower . . . Carnation. Color . . . . Blue.

Special Organization.

YELL.
Rah, Rah, Rah; Rip! Yell;
S p e c i a l.

Officers.

LUCY B. E. WILLCOX, T Z E President.
ADELINE C. TEELE, T Z E . Vice President.
WALLER I. BULLOCK, T Z E Recording Secretary.
EVELYN C. TORREY Corresponding Secretary.
DELLA MAUDE SMITH Treasurer.
MINA GOETZ . First Historian.
EMMA F. PILLING . Second Historian.
PEARL NEWMAN . Factotum.
EDITH SAWYER, T Z E
ALICE H. PURVIS . } Executive Committee.
CLARA B. FOSTER .
ALICE C. DAY, Φ Σ

Members.

BEALS, SUSIE CARY . 389 Main Street, Brockton, Mass.
BLACKWOOD, JANET L. 150 East King Street, Lancaster, Pa.
BOWEN, EVA M. Marathon, Ohio.
BULLOCK, WALLER I., T Z E 909 Cathedral Street, Baltimore, Md.
CAMP, FRANCES A. . New Britain, Conn.
CARPENTER, MABEL A. 10 Clinton Avenue, St. Johnsbury, Vt.
CASS, MARGARET A. Rochelle, Ill.
CLARKE, EDITH W. 41 Irving Place, Buffalo, N. Y.
CURRY, MINNIE C. 4 China Street, Chelsea, Mass.

DAY, ALICE C., ✻ Σ   3129 Pine Street, St. Louis, Mo.
DERRING, MARGARET R.   108 East Maxwell Street, Lexington, Ky.
DENKMANN, SUSANNE   122 Fourth Avenue, Rock Island, Ill.
EAGER, RUTH ISABEL   West Newton, Mass.
EVANS, HARRIET VIOLA   16 Park Street, Haverhill, Mass.
EVANS, JEANNIE S. S.   119 State Street, Portland, Maine.
FERGUSON, MARTHA J.   Wellesley, Mass.
FOSTER, CLARA B.   3554 Lindell Avenue, St. Louis, Mo.
GOETZ, MINA   911 Sixth Street, N. W., Washington, D. C.
GOODALL, JULIA R.   932 P Street, N. W., Washington, D. C.
HART, MARY E.   Northfield, Mass.
HASKELL, MARY E., Agora   116 East Senate Street, Columbia, S. C.
HASTINGS, MARY W.   35 Walker Avenue, Bradford, Pa.
HILL, JULIA A.   24 Monument Square, Charlestown, Mass.
HOLDEN, LULA J.   Bennington, Vt.
HOLMES, GRACE E.   39 South Street, Fitchburg, Mass.
INGALLS, M. L.   408 Gray Street, Louisville, Ky.
KELLER, MABEL   Wellesley, Mass.
LEAVITT, FANNIE M.   Newtonville, Mass.
LEE, ZAIDA B.   Oxford, N. Y.
LINCOLN, HELEN W.   22 May Street, Worcester, Mass.
LINTNER, MARY E.   Blairsville, Pa.
LIPPITT, ADDIE B   Cooperstown, N. Y.
MAY, BERTHA   Natick, Mass.
McALARNEY, ROSE W.   219 North 2d Street, Harrisburg, Pa.
MOORE, HATTIE E.   Aquebogne, New York.
NEWMAN, PEARL   Arkansas City, Kansas.
PATERSON, MARGARET JEAN   Greencastle, Ind.
PETTINGILL, FANNIE M.   Saxton's River, Vt.
PILLING, EMMA F.   Danielsonville, Conn.
PURVIS, ALICE H.   1118 13th Street, Washington, D. C.
RICHARDS, EDITH S.   897 Asylum Avenue, Hartford, Conn.
RICHARDSON, LOUISE B., Agora   Wellesley, Mass.
ROCKWELL, BERTHA   Junction City, Kansas.
ROGERS, ALICE C.   82 Commonwealth Avenue, Boston, Mass.
ROGERS, BESSIE F.   South Sudbury, Mass.
ROGERS, GRACE H.   East Derry, N. H.
RUSSELL, CARRIE L.   7 Pearl Street, Charlestown, Mass.
SAWYER, EDITH, T Z E   4 Townley Street, Hartford, Conn.
SAWYER, EDITH A.   Wiscasset, Maine.

SAWYER, LULU .   South Framingham, Mass.
SCRIBNER, BERTHA A.   Gossville, N. H.
SMITH, DELLA MAUDE   Saxton's River, Vt.
SPENCER, LOUISE   779 Asylum Avenue, Hartford, Conn.
STARR, MARGARET E., T Z E   15 Washington Street, Petersburg, Va.
STEWART, FLORA E.   Elkhorn, Wis.
STONE, RUTH W.   850 Main Street, Worcester, Mass.
SUGIYE, O TADZU   Nihara, Bingo, Hiroshima Ken, Japan.
TEELE, ADELINE C., T Z E   Curtis Street, West Somerville, Mass.
TORREY, C. EVELYN   Wellesley College, Wellesley, Mass.
TRUESDELL, MARY B.   West Stockbridge, Mass.
TURNER, ADA K.   348 Quincy Street, Brooklyn, N. Y.
UNDERWOOD, PEARL L.   145 West 58th Street, New York, N. Y.
VAN WAGENEN, HELEN M.   Oxford, N. Y.
WILLCOX, LUCY B. E., T Z E   512 Washington Boulevard, Chicago, Ill.
WOLFE, JOANNA G.   4045 Washington Boulevard, St. Louis, Mo.
WOODMAN, LIZZIE A.   Jewett City, Conn.
YATES, JENNIE O.   615 State Street, Schenectady, N. Y.

Societies
Mutually
Exclusive.

A WORD TO OUR READERS.

WE take great pleasure in recommending to our readers the following

Old and Trustworthy Firms.

We always find them attentive and anxious to please, and satisfaction is guaranteed whichever firm our readers desire to patronize.

We wish to notify the public that the remarks accompanying the trade-mark of the Shakespeare Society went in over our veto.

EDITOR IN CHIEF.

We wish to notify the public that the remarks accompanying the trade-mark of the Society Zeta Alpha went in in spite of our determined opposition.

ASSISTANT EDITOR.

We wish to notify the public that the remarks accompanying the trade-mark of the Phi Sigma Society went in in spite of our determined opposition.

FIRST LITERARY EDITOR.
THIRD LITERARY EDITOR.

We wish to notify the public that the remarks accompanying the trade-mark of the Agora went in in spite of our determined opposition.

FIRST ART EDITOR.

We wish to notify the public that the remarks accompanying the trade-mark of Tau Zeta Epsilon went in in spite of our determined opposition.

SECOND LITERARY EDITOR.
SECOND ART EDITOR.

We wish to notify the public that we upheld the action of the Editor in Chief in vetoing the remarks accompanying the trade-mark of the Shakespeare Society.

THIRD ART EDITOR.
SECOND BUSINESS MANAGER.

The Shakespeare Society.

THE Shakespeare Society of Wellesley College was founded in April, 1877. Its aim, as stated in its constitution, is "the systematic study of Shakespeare as a means for mental development." Two years later, formal connection with the London Shakespeare Society was established, and a regular correspondence with it was carried on.

The membership of the Society has usually been from thirty to forty in number. It has always held one meeting each month, at which, until '94, the members were at liberty to entertain their friends outside the Society. Since that time, however, the meetings have been closed to all except members. Since 1888 an entire play of Shakespeare has been rendered each year.

The work of the Society is literary and dramatic in character, and at each meeting representations from some of Shakespeare's plays are given. Working together in the bonds of good fellowship, the members, by their connection with the Society, come to be better scholars and better women.

Members of the Shakespeare Firm.

Officers.

Harriet M. Blake	President.
Caroline Fitz Randolph	Vice President.
Grace Miller	Recording Secretary.
Elizabeth Bartholomew	Corresponding Secretary.
S. Katherine Connor	Treasurer.
Christine Caryl	First Factotum.
Grace C. Waymouth	Second Factotum.
M. Gertrude Wilson	Keeper of the Wardrobe.

Members.

IN FACULTATE.

Sophia Jewett.
Marcia Kimball Kendall.
Mary Alice Knox.

Ellen Fitz Pendleton.
Margaret Pollock Sherwood.
Sarah Frances Whiting.

Ethel Paton.

'94.

Marion Wharton Anderson.
Elizabeth Bartholomew.
Harriet Manning Blake.
Adeline Lois Bonney.
Edith Ray Crapo.
Fannie Bradley Green.

Elisabeth Bailey Hardee.
May Lemer.
Millicent Louise Pierce.
Louis Joesephine Pope.
Caroline Fitz Randolph.
Levenia Dugan Smith.

Helen Russel Stahr.

Members of the Shakespeare Firm

CONTINUED.

'95.

Emma Christy Brooks.		Grace Miller.
Sarah Ellen Capps.		May Merrill.
Christine Caryl.		Grace Cromwell Waymouth.
Sara Katherine Connor.		Mabel Thacher Wellman.
Alice Windsor Hunt.		Mary Gertrude Wilson.
	Helen M. Kelsey.	

'96.

Elizabeth S. Adams.		Cornelia Park.
Dora E. Allen.		S. Virginia Sherwood.
Ada M. Belfield.		Elizabeth R. Snyder.
Jennie Juliet Dunbury.		Carlotta M. Swett.
	Mary L. Mudgett.	

PATRONIZED BY THE FACULTY.

Heavy Intellectual (?) Article.
We consider our Annual Spring Play a Drawing Card.

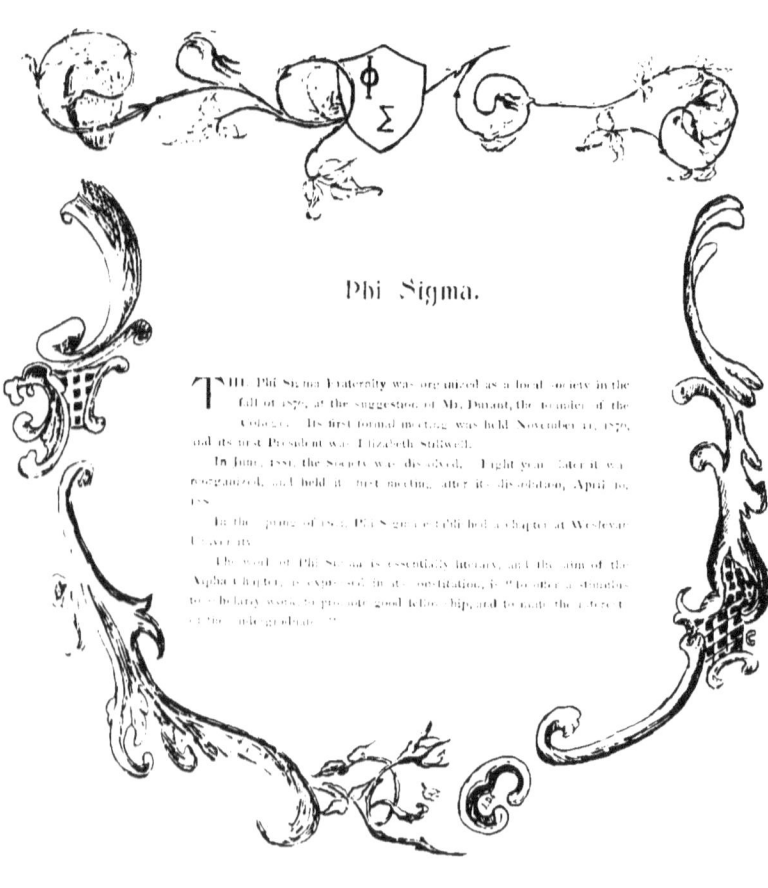

Phi Sigma.

THE Phi Sigma Fraternity was organized as a local society in the fall of 1876, at the suggestion of Mr. Durant, the founder of the College. Its first formal meeting was held November 11, 1876, and its first President was Elizabeth Stillwell.

In June, 1881, the Society was dissolved. Eight years later it was reorganized, and held its first meeting, after its dissolution, April 10, 1889.

In the spring of 1892, Phi Sigma established a chapter at Wesleyan University.

The work of Phi Sigma is essentially literary, and the aim of the Alpha Chapter, as expressed in its constitution, is "to offer a stimulus to scholarly work, to promote good fellowship, and to unite the interest of the undergraduates."

Members of the Firm Φ Σ

Places of Business.

PRINCIPAL ESTABLISHMENT . . . WELLESLEY COLLEGE.
Wellesley, Mass.

BRANCH ESTABLISHMENT . . . WESLEYAN UNIVERSITY
Middletown, Conn.

ALPHA CHAPTER.

Officers.

HELEN FOSS,	*President.*
MARION S. MITCHELL,	*Vice President.*
BERTHA E. LONGLEY,	*Recording Secretary.*
ELIZABETH A. STARK,	*Corresponding Secretary.*
GERTRUDE CARTER,	*Treasurer.*
LILLIAN E. BRANDT,	} *Marshals.*
C. LOUISE WARREN,	
EMILY B. SHULTZ,	*Editor of "Rebound."*
MARY H. HOLMES,	*Critic.*

Members.

IN FACULTATE.

KATHARINE LEE BATES.
ISABEL GRAVES.

ANNIE SYBIL MONTAGUE.
SARAH WOODMAN PAUL.

'91.

MAY D. NEWCOMB.

Members of the Firm Φ Σ

CONTINUED.

'92.
M. GERTRUDE CUSHING.

'94.

SARA BURROWES.   MARION S. MITCHELL.
HELEN FOSS.   EMILIE W. PORTER.
MARY H. HOLMES.   ETHEL STANWOOD.
EDITH JUDSON.   EMILY B. SHULTZ.

BERTHA E. LONGLEY.

'95.

LILLIAN E. BRANDT.   CAROLINE W. JACOBUS.
MARY G. CANNON.   HELEN JAMES.
GERTRUDE CARTER.   L. MAY PITKIN.
MARY E. CHASE.   ELIZABETH A. STARK.
MABEL E. DAVIDSON.   C. LOUISE WARREN.

'96.

HARRIET R. BALDWIN.   ALICE H. SCHOULER.
HELEN M. DUDLEY.   CLARA VON WETTBERG.
THERESA L. HUNTINGTON.   ANNA C. WITHERLE.
JULIA H. LYMAN.   MARY WOODIN.

FRANCES K. PULLEN.

'97.
MARY WANAMAKER MILLER.

SPECIAL.
ALICE DAY.

ACTIVE AND ENTERPRISING AGENTS IN ALL PARTS OF THE COLLEGE.

We have done a rushing business all the year, and expect the rush to continue until Commencement. Our departments are varied, and we aim to excel in each.

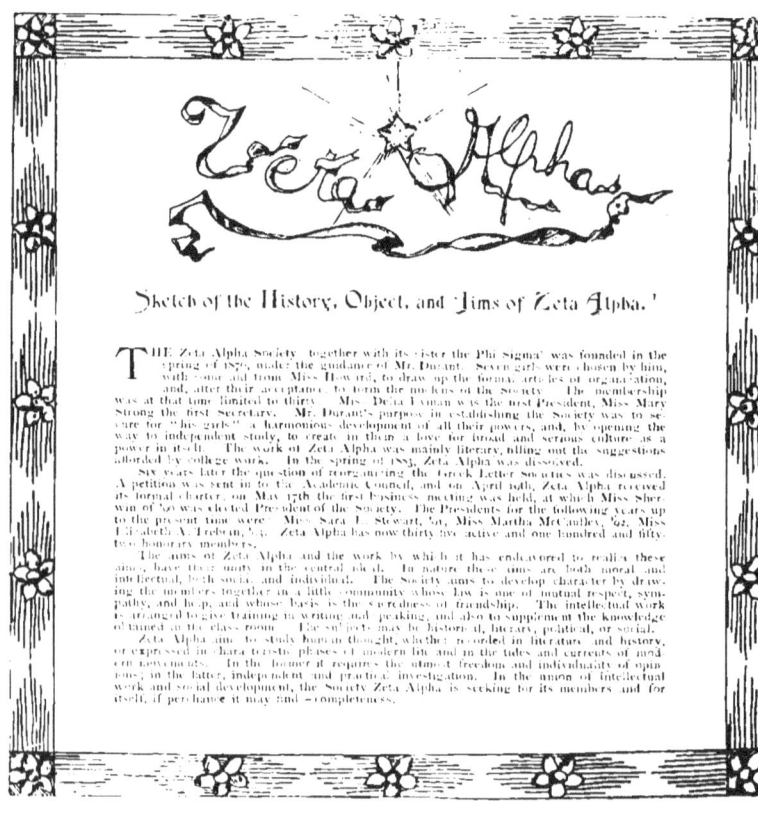

Sketch of the History, Object, and Aims of Zeta Alpha.

THE Zeta Alpha Society, together with its sister the Phi Sigma, was founded in the spring of 1876, under the guidance of Mr. Durant. Seven girls were chosen by him, with some aid from Miss Howard, to draw up the formal articles of organization, and, after their acceptance, to form the nucleus of the Society. The membership was at that time limited to thirty. Miss Delia Lyman was the first President, Miss Mary Strong the first Secretary. Mr. Durant's purpose in establishing the Society was to secure for "his girls" a harmonious development of all their powers, and, by opening the way to independent study, to create in them a love for broad and serious culture as a power in itself. The work of Zeta Alpha was mainly literary, filling out the suggestions afforded by college work. In the spring of 1883, Zeta Alpha was dissolved.

Six years later the question of reorganizing the Greek Letter Societies was discussed. A petition was sent in to the Academic Council, and on April 19th, Zeta Alpha received its formal charter, on May 17th the first business meeting was held, at which Miss Sherwin of '90 was elected President of the Society. The Presidents for the following years up to the present time were: Miss Sara L. Stewart, '91, Miss Martha McCaulley, '92, Miss Elizabeth A. Treebern, '93. Zeta Alpha has now thirty-five active and one hundred and fifty-two honorary members.

The aims of Zeta Alpha and the work by which it has endeavored to realize these aims, have their unity in the central ideal. In nature these aims are both moral and intellectual, both social, and individual. The Society aims to develop character by drawing the members together in a little community whose law is one of mutual respect, sympathy, and help, and whose basis is the sacredness of friendship. The intellectual work is arranged to give training in writing and speaking, and also to supplement the knowledge obtained in the class-room. The subjects may be historical, literary, political, or social. Zeta Alpha aims to study human thought, whether recorded in literature and history, or expressed in characteristic phases of modern life and in the tides and currents of modern movements. In the former it requires the utmost freedom and individuality of opinions; in the latter, independent and practical investigation. In the union of intellectual work and social development, the Society Zeta Alpha is seeking for its members and for itself, if perchance it may find — completeness.

Members of the Firm Z A

Officers.

JULIA S. BUFFINGTON	*President.*
MARION CANFIELD	*Vice President.*
KATE W. NELSON	*Recording Secretary.*
MARY LOUISE BOSWELL	*Corresponding Secretary.*
CLARA M. KRUSE	*Treasurer.*
WINIFRED AUGSBURY	*First Marshal.*
CLARA L. WILLIS	*Second Marshal.*
ALICE W. KELLOGG	*Editor of "The True Blue."*

Members.

IN FACULTATE.

ELLEN L. BURRELL.   CHARLOTTE FITCH ROBERTS.

'94.

L. GERTRUDE ANGEL.	MARY KEYT ISHAM.
ANNA H. BLAUVELT.	ALICE W. KELLOGG.
MARY L. BOSWELL.	CLARA M. KRUSE.
JULIA S. BUFFINGTON.	MARY MILLARD.
MARION CANFIELD.	MIRIAM NEWCOMBE.
KATHERINE R. COLLINS.	MARY J. SALTER.
MARY K. CONYNGTON.	ELIZABETH M. WOOD.

HELEN P. DRAKE.

Members of the Firm Z A

CONTINUED.

'95.

GRACE L. ADDEMAN.
WINIFRED M. AUGSBURY.
HELEN N. BLAKESLEE.
HELEN DENNISS.
MARY E. FIELD.
FLORENCE T. FORBES.

ADAH M. HASBROOK.
CORNELIA S. HUNTINGTON.
EDITH JONES.
ALETHEA LEDYARD.
KATE W. NELSON.
ELIZABETH PEALE.

'96.

EMILY H. BROWN.
AGNES L. CALDWELL.
LUCY J. FREEMAN.

MARY HEFFERAN.

MARY MONTGOMERY.
VIRGINIA A. SCHOONOVER.
MARTHA H. SHACKFORD.

'97.

M. DENISON WILT.

SPECIAL.

PEARL UNDERWOOD.

OUR WELL-KNOWN MODESTY FORBIDS LENGTHY
REFERENCE TO OUR MERITS.

We wish, however, to call attention to our business-like habit of publishing annually a list of our incoming stock.

Tau Zeta Epsilon

THE Society now known as Tau Zeta Epsilon was started in 1889. It had long been evident to certain earnest college students that a busy academic life, removed from the more stirring interests of the world, is but too apt to degenerate into a meaningless routine, devoid of much that makes life beautiful. Consequently they formed themselves into an organization known as the "Art Club," for the study of the beautiful in Art, the membership being open to any desiring it. Later, the "Art Club" became a more formal organization, with restricted membership, mutually exclusive with the other Wellesley societies, and was known as the "Art Society," the *raison d'être* being the study of the beautiful wherever found, whether in the realms of painting, sculpture, architecture, music, or literature. Beauty was the guide, and the whole wide world a studio. Then the social life of the society was emphasized, the members drew together in a closer bond, and a society home was established in the Art Building. Finally it became evident that again had the organization outgrown its name, and the more distinctive title Tau Zeta Epsilon was adopted.

Members of the Firm T Z E

Officers.

JANE WILLIAMS	*President.*
RUBY P. BRIDGMAN	*Vice President.*
EFFIE McMILLAN	*Recording Secretary.*
HELEN McMILLAN	*Corresponding Secretary.*
GRACE O. EDWARDS	*Treasurer.*
ALBERTA M. WELCH	*Keepers.*
CHARLOTTE GOODRICH	

Members.

HONORARY.

Mr. A. W. STETSON. Mr. MARTIN BRIMMER.

Professor CHARLES ELIOT NORTON.

IN FACULTATE.

ELIZABETH H. DENIO. ANNE EUGENIA MORGAN.

'92.

MAUDE RYLANDS KELLER.

'94.

RUBY PORTER BRIDGMAN.	EFFIE McMILLAN.
FANNIE CHRISTINE BROOKS.	HELEN McMILLAN.
GRACE OSBORNE EDWARDS.	EDNA FRANCES PRESSEY.
ANNETTE FINNIGAN.	JANE WILLIAMS.
HARRIET ALICE FRIDAY.	ALICE I. WOOD.

Members of the Firm T Z E

CONTINUED.

'95.

FRANCES BLANCHE ARTER.
FANNIE ESTELLE AUSTIN.

CHARLOTTE GOODRICH.

ALICE WHITNEY NORCROSS.
ALBERTA MAUDE WELCH.

'96.

MAY E. KELLOGG.

CAROLINE W. KING.

LYDIA K. WILKINS.

SPECIALS.

WALTER I. BULLOCK.
EDITH SAWYER.

ADELINE TEELE.
LUCY E. B. WILLCOX.

SUCCESSORS TO THE ART SOCIETY.

We do the same old business at the same old stand. Though our outward symbols may change, our (he)Art is ever the same.

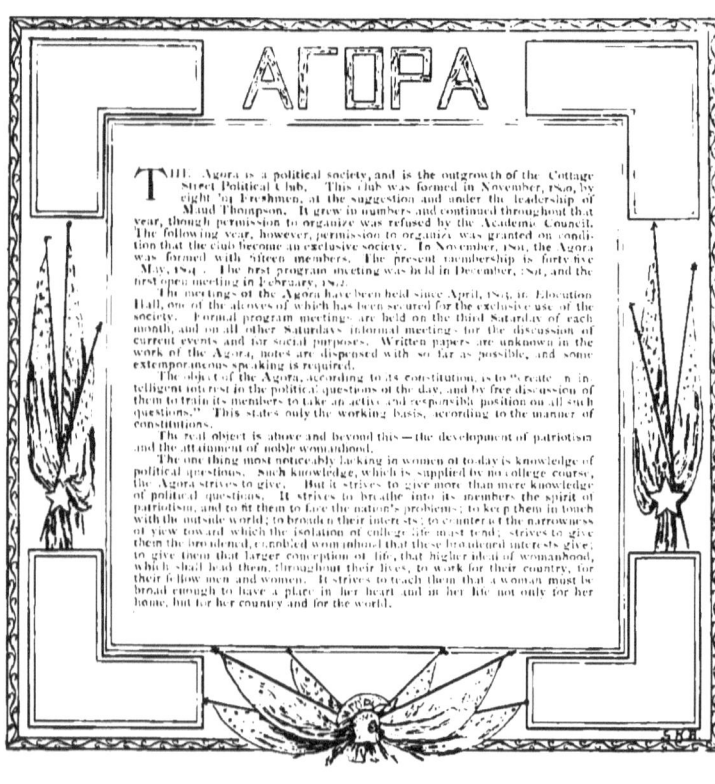

ΑΓΟΡΑ

THE Agora is a political society, and is the outgrowth of the Cottage Street Political Club. This club was formed in November, 1889, by eight of freshmen, at the suggestion and under the leadership of Maud Thompson. It grew in numbers and continued throughout that year, though permission to organize was refused by the Academic Council. The following year, however, permission to organize was granted on condition that the club become an exclusive society. In November, 1891, the Agora was formed with fifteen members. The present membership is forty-five May, 1894. The first program meeting was held in December, 1891, and the first open meeting in February, 1892.

The meetings of the Agora have been held since April, 1893, in Education Hall, one of the alcoves of which has been secured for the exclusive use of the society. Formal program meetings are held on the third Saturday of each month, and on all other Saturdays informal meetings for the discussion of current events and for social purposes. Written papers are unknown in the work of the Agora, notes are dispensed with so far as possible, and some extemporaneous speaking is required.

The object of the Agora, according to its constitution, is to "create an intelligent interest in the political questions of the day, and by free discussion of them to train its members to take an active and responsible position on all such questions." This states only the working basis, according to the manner of constitutions.

The real object is above and beyond this — the development of patriotism and the attainment of noble womanhood.

The one thing most noticeably lacking in women of to-day is knowledge of political questions. Such knowledge, which is supplied by no college course, the Agora strives to give. But it strives to give more than mere knowledge of political questions. It strives to breathe into its members the spirit of patriotism, and to fit them to face the nation's problems; to keep them in touch with the outside world; to broaden their interests; to counteract the narrowness of view toward which the isolation of college life must tend; strives to give them the broadened, ennobled womanhood that these broadened interests give; to give them that larger conception of life, that higher ideal of womanhood, which shall lead them, throughout their lives, to work for their country, for their fellow men and women. It strives to teach them that a woman must be broad enough to have a place in her heart and in her life not only for her home, but for her country and for the world.

Members of the Political Firm.

Officers.

ABIGAIL H. LAUGHLIN	*President.*
ELVA H. YOUNG	*Vice President.*
CAROLINE W. FIELD	*Recording Secretary.*
ORA W. L. SLATER	*Corresponding Secretary.*
MARY S. YOUNG	*Treasurer.*
ARLINE H. SMITH	*Sergeant-at-Arms.*
SARAH C. WEED	} *Executive Committee.*
SARAH H. BIXBY	

Members.

IN FACULTATE.

MARY WHITON CALKINS.   KATHERINE COMAN.

CARLA WENCKEBACH.

'94.

ELIZA ABIAH BATEMAN.   ELEANORE NEVA KELLOGG.
SARAH CLARISSA WHITE BENSON.   ABIGAIL HILL LAUGHLIN.
SARAH HATHAWAY BIXBY.   MABEL WOODBURY LEAROYD.
LUCY PEARCE BROWNELL.   STELLA MORRIS OSGOOD.
SARAH JULIA BURGESS.   ANNA KATRINA PETERSON.
CAROLINE WILLIAMS FIELD.   ORA WINONA LOUISE SLATER.
SUSAN SHELDON HAWLEY.   FLORENCE MARTIN TOBEY.
HELEN RUTH HIBBARD.   ANNIE LOUISE VINAL.
BERTHA CHRISTINE JACKSON.   MARY LOUISE WETHERBEE.

Members of the Political Firm

CONTINUED.

'95.

CLARA MANTER BENSON.
HELEN MABEL BISBEE.
MARY GRACE CALDWELL.
CECELIA DICKIE.
KATHERINE FACKENTHAL.

MARY LILIAN JONES.
MARY DAVIS PRIOR.
ARLINE HOPGOOD SMITH.
MARTHA T. WATERMAN.
SARAH CHAMBERLAIN WEED.

MARY SOPHIA YOUNG.

'96.

ALBERTA FRANCES BAKER.
BELINDA MILES BOGARDUS.
ANNIE EUGENIA COBB.
HELENA DE COU.
SARAH LOUISE HADLEY.

JOANNA STODDARD PARKER.
ANNA HAMLIN PEAKS.
EDITH MOSS RHOADES.
CORA E. STODDARD.
ELVA HURLBURT YOUNG.

ANNE ELIZABETH ZIEGLER.

SPECIALS.

MARY E. HASKELL.

LOUISE S. RICHARDSON.

WE ARE THE PEOPLE!!!

New ourselves we keep — with all the novelties
Flags given away free at our winter opening. All of
carried away by a Gale of enthusiasm.

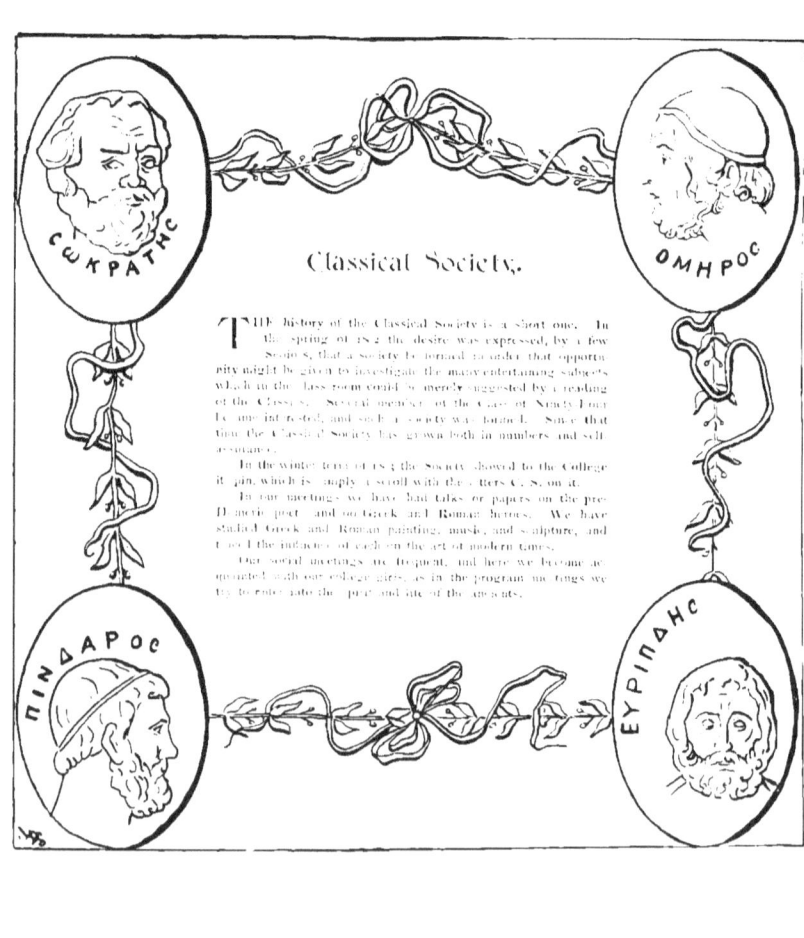

Members of the Classical Firm.

Officers.

Florence W. Davis	*President.*
Grace H. Perkins	*Vice President.*
Anna G. Chute	*Recording Secretary.*
Grace C. Albee	*Corresponding Secretary.*
Mary E. Chapin	
Jeannette A. Moulton	} *Executive Committee.*
Margaret B. Simmons	
Ida M. Brooks	} *Factotums.*
Beatrice Stepanek	

Members.

IN FACULTATE.

Angie Clara Chapin.

'93.

Mabel A. Hayes.

'94.

Carolyn J. Peck.

Grace C. Albee.　　　　　　　　　　Grace H. Perkins.
Florence W. Davis.　　　　　　　　　Lillian B. Quinby.
Jeannette A. Moulton.　　　　　　　Blanche L. Thayer.

Members of the Classical Firm

CONTINUED.

'95.

IDA M. BROOKS.		NELLIE J. STIMPSON.
MARY E. CHAPIN.		BEATRICE STEPANEK.
ANNA G. CHUTE.		MARGARET B. SIMMONS.
	ANNIE M. LEONARD.	

'96.

IRENE KAHN.		GRACE B. TOWNSEND.
	MABEL F. RAND.	

*SMALL BUT EXCLUSIVE

Careful attention paid to all matters of classical interest, including the subjects of Gothic and modern American Architecture.

* These remarks went in with the unanimous consent of the Board. — EDITOR.

* An Amœba, the lowest form of animal life.

Organizations.

Christian Association.

Officers.

FRANCES E. LORD.	*President.*
HELEN DENNIS, '95	*Vice President.*
GERTRUDE L. DENNIS, '96	*Recording Secretary.*
CAROLINE W. FIELD, '94	*Corresponding Secretary.*
ROXANA H. VIVIAN, '94	*Treasurer.*

Chairmen.

ALICE W. KELLOGG, '94	*Missionary Committee.*
SARAH H. BIXBY, '94	*Temperance Committee.*
ELEANORE N. KELLOGG, '94	*Indian Committee.*
JULIA S. BURGESS, '94	*General Religious Work Committee.*
HARRIET M. BLAKE, '94	*Reception Committee.*
ANNIE S. MONTAGUE	*Devotional Committee.*

Student Volunteers.

Officers.

Mabel W. Learoyd, '94 . . . . Chairman.
Katherine Fackenthal, '95 . . . . Secretary.
Iza B. Skelton, '95 .
Sarah C. Weed, '95 . } Executive Committee.
Ada May Krecker, '95

The Wellesley Chapter of the College Settlements Association.

Officers.

Helen M. Kelsey, '95 . . . . President.
Katherine Coman, Faculty
Edith R. Crapo, '94 .
Helen James, '95 . } Vice Presidents.
Cora E. Stoddard, '96
Gertrude Rushmore, '97 .
Bertha Scribner, Sp.
Alice W. Kellogg, '94 . . . . Secretary and Treasurer.

Membership, 145.

Publications.

EDITORIAL BOARD

Wellesley Publications.

The Legenda.
PUBLISHED ANNUALLY BY THE SENIOR CLASS.

The Wellesley Magazine.

Editors for '93-'94.

MARY K. CONYNGTON, '94. *Editor in Chief.*
ANNA K. PETERSON, '94.   *Associate Editor.*

Business Managers.
HELEN R. STAHR, '94.   FLORENCE M. TOBEY, '94.

Literary Editors.
ALICE W. KELLOGG, '94.   LILIAN B. QUINBY, '94.
EMILY B. SHULTZ, '94.   MARY K. ISHAM, '94.
                    MAUDE R. KELLER, '92.
                    LOUISE RICHARDSON, Sp.

L. GERTRUDE ANGELL . . . . . *Address of Welcome.*
ANNA KATRINA PETERSON . . . *Orator.*
ALICE WELCH KELLOGG . . . . *Address to Undergraduates.*
JULIA STEVENS BUFFINGTON . . *Poet.*
CAROLINE FITZ RANDOLPH . . . *Mistress of Ceremonies.*

Aids.

EDITH RAY CRAPO.   EVANGELINE L. SHERWOOD.
ADELINE LOIS BONNEY.   ELIZABETH MORRIS WOOD.
EDITH JUDSON.   MABEL WOODBURY LEAROYD.

'96.

AGNES LOUISE CALDWELL . . . . . *Giver of Spade.*

'97.

MARGARETTE D. PURINGTON . . . *Orator.*
HELEN WEBSTER PETTEE . . . . *Receiver of Spade.*
ETHELBERTA HASBROUK . . . . . *Mistress of Ceremonies.*

Aids.

EDITH HELEN LADD.   MARY BESSIE GATES.
MARY KATHERINE PINKHAM.   RUTH C. WILLIS.

140

Beethoven Society.

Officers.

ALETHEA LEDYARD, '95	*President.*
LUCY E. B. WILLCOX, Sp.	*Vice President.*
KATHERINE FACKENTHAL, '95	*Recording Secretary.*
EDITH SAWYER, Sp.	*Corresponding Secretary.*
MAY BELLE WILLIS, '95	*Treasurer.*
ETHEL HOWARD, '96	} *Factotums.*
BESSIE G. PIERCE, '96	

JUNIUS W. HILL, Director.

Wellesley College Glee Club.

Officers.

FLORENCE T. FORBES	*President.*
EDITH SAWYER	*Leader.*
MARY E. CHAPIN	*Business Manager.*
ELLEN M. CUSHING	*Librarian.*
SUSIE CARY BEALS	*Accompanist.*

JUNIUS W. HILL, Director.

First Sopranos.

KATE W. NELSON, '95.	EMILY H. BROWN, '96.
JOSEPHINE H. BATCHELDER, '96.	JENNIE O. YATES, Sp.

Second Sopranos.

ELIZABETH M. WOOD, '94.	FRANCES G. HOYT, '98.
F. BLANCHE ARTER, '95.	PEARL NEWMAN, MUS.

First Altos.

MARY E. CHAPIN, '95.	MARY W. MONTGOMERY, '96.
ELLEN M. CUSHING, '96.	EDITH SAWYER, MUS.

Second Altos.

MABEL W. LEAROYD, '94.	MABEL F. RAND, '96.
FLORENCE T. FORBES, '95.	LULA J. HOLDEN, Sp.

WELLESLEY COLLEGE BANJO CLUB.

Wellesley College Banjo Club.

Officers.

MARION CANFIELD . . . . President.
MABEL KELLER . . . . Leader.
WINIFRED AUGSBURY . . . . . . Business Manager.
DORA ALLEN . . . . Factotum.

Banjeurines.

MARION CANFIELD, '94.   MAY B. WILLIS, '95.
ARTEMISIA STONE, '94.   MABEL KELLER, Mus.

First Banjos.

MAY ALLEN, '97.   FLORENCE PAINTER, '97.

Second Banjos.

HELEN JAMES, '95.   ETHEL HASBROOK, '97.

Guitars.

WINIFRED AUGSBURY, '95.   FLORENCE S. SHIRLEY, '95.
BESSIE S. SMITH, '95.   GRACE WOODIN, '95.
                DORA E. ALLEN, '96.

146

Outdoor Sports and Pastimes.

A Playstead for the use of this department is in process of preparation.
A conference, composed of committees from the several classes, together with Miss Lucile Eaton Hill, Director of the Department of Physical Training, have in charge the Outdoor Sports and Pastimes. They have passed the following regulations:—

I. The Outdoor Sports and Pastimes shall be in connection with the Department of Physical Training.

II. The classes shall all be represented in these Outdoor Sports and Pastimes by crews, teams, and clubs.

III. There shall be a Field Day, or Field Days, on which inter-class matches shall be played.

IV. These clubs, crews, and teams shall unite to form a Sports and Pastimes Association.

The candidates for all crews, teams, and clubs are selected according to the recommendations of the Physical Examiner, and according to the grade of work done in the Gymnasium.

In connection with this department there are already formed the following crews, teams, and clubs:—

1. Class Crews.
2. Class Basket Ball Teams.
3. Tennis Club.
4. Bicycle Club.
5. Golf Club.
6. Pedestrian Club.

Visiting Committee of Department of Physical Training.

DR. HAROLD WILLIAMS, *Chairman*	. Boston.
EX-GOV. W. E. RUSSELL .	Cambridge.
MR. ASTOR CARY .	. Boston.
DR. WALTER CHANNING .	Brookline.
DR. E. M. HARTWELL .	. Boston.

Capacity of Lungs.

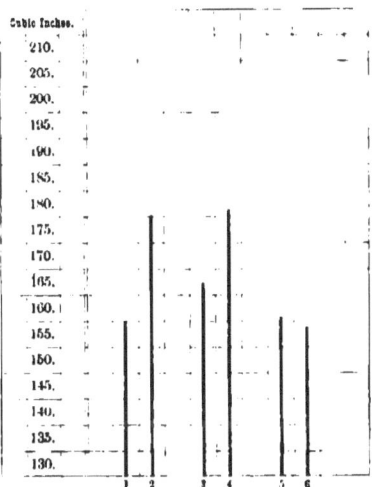

1. Mean lung capacity of the Class Crews, November, 1892.
2. Mean lung capacity of the Class Crews, May, 1893.
   (Five months' training in the Gymnasium; one month on the Lake.)
3. Mean lung capacity of 20 students, November, 1892.
4. Mean lung capacity of 20 students, May, 1893.
   Five months of required Swedish Gymnastics.)
5. Mean lung capacity of 20 students, November, 1892.
6. Mean lung capacity of 20 students, May, 1893.
   (Receiving NO physical training.)

Strength of Back.

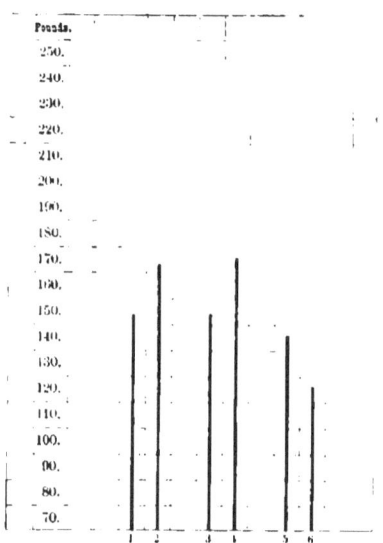

1. Mean strength of back of the Class Crews, November, 1892.
2. Mean strength of back of the Class Crews, May, 1893.
   Five months' training in the Gymnasium; one month on the Lake.
3. Mean strength of back of 20 students, November, 1892.
4. Mean strength of back of 20 students, May, 1893.
   Five months of required Swedish Gymnastics.
5. Mean strength of back of 20 students, November, 1892.
6. Mean strength of back of 20 students, May, 1893.
   Receiving NO physical training.

Bicycle Club.

Officers.

Eleanor Stephenson, '95	President.
Abby F. Blanchard, '97	Vice President.
Alice H. Purvis, Sp.	Secretary and Treasurer.
Carla Wenckebach	Captain.
Ada M. Clark	First Lieutenant.
Grace E. Jarvis	Second Lieutenant.
Isabelle H. Fiske	Business Manager.

Tennis Association.

Officers.

Mabel Clara Dodge	President.
Alice Windsor Hunt	Vice President.
Cora E. Stoddard	Recording Secretary.
Mary Frazer Smith	Treasurer.
Edith Ray Crapo	
C. Louise Warren	Executive Committee.
May E. Kellogg	

NINETY-FOUR CREW AND SUBSTITUTES

Class Crews.

Ninety-Four Crew and Substitutes.

Boat, Wabanannung (Star of the East).

MARION CANFIELD, *Captain and Stroke.*

MABEL W. LEAROYD, *Coxswain.*

ISABELLE CAMPBELL.
MARION CANFIELD.
ELEANOR CHACE.
GRACE EDWARDS.
EFFIE MACMILLAN.
HELEN MACMILLAN.

LAURA MALLOON.
EDNA PRESSEY.
THEODORA SKIDMORE.
HELEN STAHR.
ARTEMESIA STONE.
ALICE I. WOOD.

Ninety-Five Crew and Substitutes.

Boat, Soangataha (Strong-hearted).

MARY CANNON, *Captain and Stroke*.
MAY MERRILL, *Coxswain*.

MARY CANNON.
SYBIL BOYNTON.
E. CHRISTY BROOKS.
MARY CHASE.
HELEN DENNIS.
FRANCES HILDRETH.

ADAH HASBROOK.
ALICE HUNT.
FLORA KRUM.
MAY MERRILL.
ELIZABETH STARK.
GRACE WOODIN.

Ninety-Six Crew and Substitutes.

Boat, Loch Learoch (Water-bird).

THERESA HUNTINGTON, *Captain and Stroke*.
CLARA KEENE, *Coxswain*.

AMY BOUTELLE.
MARTHA BULLIS.
EDITH BUTLER.
HELEN CHANDLER.
ELLEN CUSHING.
EMMA GEYER.
GRACE GODFREY.
THERESA HUNTINGTON.

CLARA KEENE.
AMY LANE.
MARY MONTGOMERY.
GRACE NUTTER.
ELIZABETH SNYDER.
CARLOTTA SWETT.
MARY WITCHER.
EDITH WYLIE.

Special Crew and Substitutes.

Boat . . . Tupelo.

MABEL KELLER, *Captain and Stroke.*
PEARL NEWMAN, *Coxswain.*

EVA BOWEN.
MARGARET CASS.
CLARA FOSTER.
JEANETTE FERGUSON.
MARY HASTINGS.
MABEL KELLER.

CAROLYN LORD.
PEARL NEWMAN.
ALICE PURVIS.
BERTHA ROCKWELL.
FLORA STEWART.
MARGARET STARR.

O thou foolish Freshman who nibblest
much of Huyler's;

O thou heedless Sophomore who takest
not thy daily walk;

O thou reckless Junior who sittest up
late o' nights,—

See to what a pass thou wilt come if
thou turnest not from thy evil way!

O thou poor Senior who hast committed
all these sinful deeds, and who hast
had no saving training of the gymnasium sort, see what thou art!

O thou pitying reader, who hast gold,

**PLEASE DIE AND
GIVE US A GYMNASIUM.**

Editorials.

TO one who has never tried it, the publication of a LEGENDA, consisting merely of class lists and new and original ideas, may seem an easy matter. When we first entered upon that task we felt that, although not altogether easy, it was certainly possible. This was nine months ago. Since then we have learned a great deal. We have found that the class lists may be obtained with fair accuracy, but we have no longer any delusion about new and original ideas. We have grasped the fact that they are impossibilities. Our first bit of enlightenment in this direction came when, confiding to a fellow-editor what we supposed to be a bright, new idea of our own, we were informed, with surprise and indignation, that the idea was hers, and had been imparted to us for consideration some days before. This was discouraging, but we did not give up. With a childlike faith—which in the light of our later experience seems truly pathetic—we went on producing idea after idea, and carefully writing each one down, so as not to forget it, we would communicate them to our fellow-editors amid enthusiastic congratulations. And then we would go away and find those same ideas in all sorts of places: some would turn up in preceding LEGENDAS, others in daily papers, and others in the works of classic writers; some dated back to Adam, and others, as far as we could discover, were only as old as Homer. After a while we scarcely dared to open a book of any kind, for fear of finding one of our ideas in it. We went on, however, in the mad search for the original until we were completely worn out; then we turned to the class lists. Oh, the relief of those lists! The names had been selected, combined, and even spelt for us; no need of originality here — originality would be actually out of place. It is to those class lists that we now point with pride as the really creditable feature of the book; and for those who scoff at the absence of original ideas, we have only pity: we know by what painful experience they must attain to the knowledge that there is no such thing as an original idea.

✻

SINCE the eventful evening when the resignation of the LEGENDA BOARD was so conspicuous by its absence, we have been sailing under false colors. In the pages of this book, the product of our labors, the everlasting memorial, not only of our willingness to serve our

Class and our College, but also of our ability to do it, we desire to make public confession of the wherefore of our not resigning. It was not modesty that restrained us; not a desire to escape the tolling of the silver iterance of class appreciation; nor was it the love of peace, expressed by refraining to add more fuel to the fire of Class elections; nor was it a spirit of love, a desire to do unto others as we would have them do unto us; nay, none of these,—but a business contract with our printer!

※

On April 16th the LEGENDA goes to press. On April 17th the LEGENDA BOARD anticipate drawing a long breath; we may even find time to bow to our friends in the corridor. On April 18th we expect to go to chapel, and those of us who have not more than two papers the next week are extravagant enough to hope to do a little necessary mending. Then, perhaps, as the editor sits quietly musing over some long-forgotten shoe button, suddenly there will come to her mind an idea whose brilliancy would have made '94's LEGENDA a shining light for ages to come; or, as she blows the dust off of her neglected books, a joke will rise up before her, fresh and original as the first pun made in Eden. Or, while the Art editor peacefully weaves conventional designs into the heel of a stocking, there will dawn upon her a conception whose beauty is only surpassed by its novelty. But all in vain come the crowding thoughts, merry, and new, and bright: time and the printer stay for naught. The ideas which might have been the glory and the crown of our LEGENDA will sink back into the oblivion whence they came, or else be ignominiously chopped up "to coldly furnish forth" a week of daily themes. Such is fate! But then, perhaps it might make us conceited if the LEGENDA had been any brighter than it is.

※ ※ ※

We have noted with some astonishment that although the Class of '94 counts among its members many ardent advocates of equal rights, it has not carried out this principle in the matter of Senior privileges. We have but to turn to the coast of Connecticut, or the Jersey jungle where the Tiger roams, to behold our brothers of the cap and gown spinning their tops and trundling their hoops with all the dignity and self-satisfaction which only a Senior privilege can confer. But we sit here in the darkness of oppressed womanhood, classed by the law with children and idiots, with no tops, no hoops, no marbles,—nothing to show to the world our intellectual advancement. We would, therefore, propose that henceforth the jumping-rope be the accompaniment of the cap and gown at Wellesley. We should thus prove beyond all question our right to stand shoulder to shoulder with the men of our generation; and, moreover, on the æsthetic side, add an attraction to the College. What could be more picturesque than the graceful flow of the gown as its wearer soared over the rope? Indeed, we can imagine nothing more impressive than the campus, of a pleasant afternoon, covered with a hundred or more "sweet girl graduates" in varying poses of airy flight. Since '94 has failed to take this step in the progress of Wellesley's development, let '95, as soon as the new gowns arrive, add this reform to the long list of her glorious deeds.

※

How long will ye try our patience, O delinquents? How long will your selfishness provoke our fury? Do neither daily notices, nor earnest pleading, nor threatenings, nor even the tears of the foragers and factotums, move you? Can nothing induce you to attend Class meetings, O ye lazy and thoughtless maidens? Many have been the evenings we have urged you to come; many have been the night watches we have waited in vain for the seats to be filled which your absence made vacant. *O tempora! O mores!* Neither time nor eternity can wipe from our memory the vivid remembrance of those weary and sleepy seasons.

Where were you the first night, last night, and all the intervening nights, while we were waiting for you? Are you aware that the assembled company of students knew what you were doing on those nights? Knew that in your absence you were calmly planning their destruction? Their destruction, I say; for by your absence were you not stealing from them their precious moments, the loss of which caused their annihilation, their failure, their flunks, in the duties of the morrow?

O dii immortales! Would that some power in heaven or on earth could show you the error of your way! Would that you could be made to turn from your path of evil! Take warning while still there is time, before the destruction which you prepare for others be brought upon yourself. Show no longer this unequaled selfishness! Do ye, each and all, show your loyalty to your Class and College by prompt attendance at every meeting!

※ ※ ※

WE, the Business Editors of the '94 LEGENDA, on completing our last task in its behalf, humbly offer sundry words of counsel to those who, undertaking the management of the next LEGENDA, will assume our responsibilities. From our recent experience with the business world we have gleaned various bits of useful knowledge, by the recital of which we hope to forewarn and to forearm you : —

  I. Begin early in your Senior year (or before, if possible) to know
    1. The Printer.
    2. The Advertising Agent.
    3. The Photographer.

  This does not mean merely to be acquainted with an individual in each profession, but to know the type of such a person; in short, know what a printer *is*, and what an advertising agent is, or can be.
    N. B.—Learn any little eccentricities to which the latter class is subject.

  II. Know what it is to make a book,—as to size, thickness, color, print, engraving, advertising, and COST.
    N. B.—To elect a course in domestic work in any department, the head of which is expecting to issue a book, will be the best way to get plenty of experience with every little detail in such matters.

  III. Know the nature of contracts.
    N. B.—Take a course in Political Economy, if necessary. If not possible, any lecture after chapel on not keeping appointments may help indirectly.

  IV. Show to what degree a true college student can make a good business woman by her promptness in keeping engagements, accuracy in business transactions, and general business-like demeanor.
    N. B.—Any previous training in correspondence, typewriting or bookkeeping will be of inestimable value in accomplishing this end.

  And now, oh '95 ! if you will but study thoroughly these suggestions, pursue the preliminary courses of study here prescribed, and, above all, read carefully all the advertisements in our LEGENDA, we feel that your success is assured; nay, more, we hope, and confidently expect, that you will make money enough, and be unselfish enough after you have made it, to build us a new Chapel, or to complete the Boathouse Fund.

College Calendar.

4. The grind begins once more.
6. We observe Fast Day.
7. A request is received from an admirer of '95 to name his new hair restorer "The Wellesley College Sweet Pea Hair Lotion." [Fact.]
9. Dr. J. Heinston, of Brooklyn, preaches in the Chapel.
   New gowns.
10. Commissioner Morgan speaks on the Indian question.
12. In bookstore ; member of department of Mathematics : " How much are the matches?" " Three cents a box." " I want three boxes. How much is that, please?"
16. Dr. W. H. Thomas, of Lowell, preaches in the Chapel.
17. Junior social to Freshmen.
19. Professor of Literature to self-possessed Junior : " What are the author's views on this subject. Miss ——?" " I have not reached that point; I have not quite finished the essay." " Ah, you began at the end and read backward? This is on the first page."
20. The young lady who thinks the soles of shoes are made of wood, decides to make herself a new spring gown of green and purple crinoline.
23. Prof. E. B. Andrews, of Brown University, preaches in the Chapel.
24. Lecture on Tennyson, with readings by Prof. Bliss Perry, of Williams College.
   Forensic subjects posted:—
   I. Is domestic work a cause for moral degeneracy on the part of the students?
   II. Does strict veracity prevail in the letters written by the Sophomores to the Professor of Elocution?

III. Is it therapeutically scientific to differentiate the active principle from the crude drug in medicine?
IV. Should the library be used as a place for social gatherings?
V. Should the College confer a degree upon students who omit meals to grind?
VI. Is the algo-fungal theory of lichens tenable?
VII. Has the atmosphere of Wellesley fossilizing properties?
VIII. Is the five-o'clock prayer meeting at Stone Hall justifiable?
IX. Ought not the Agora, as an organization which favors political reform, to be opposed to the Swett-ing system?

30. Prof. H. A. Frink, of Amherst College, preaches in the Chapel.

1. Waban party.
   The Faculty entertain '93.
5. Soangetaha christened to the tune of "Champagne Charlie."
6. Ninety-Six's first class social. Everything suited to their age and intelligence.
7. Dr. William H. Willcox, of Malden, preaches in the Chapel.
8. Mr. Jacob A. Riis, of New York, lectures on "The Children of the Poor."
   Instructor in Hebrew: "But I should not have interrupted you, Miss ——; *perhaps* you were going to say something to the point."
14. Rev. H. P. Dewey, of Concord, N. H., preaches in the Chapel.
15. Ninety-Five plants maple (alias sycamore) number two.
21. Dr. William H. Willcox, of Malden, preaches in the Chapel.
22. Junior Temperance Debate.
    The Faculty at home to '94. (Great run on excuse blanks.)
25. Professor: "I really must be going to my office hours; they have already been going on twenty minutes without me."
27. Shakespeare play.
29. Glee Club Concert.

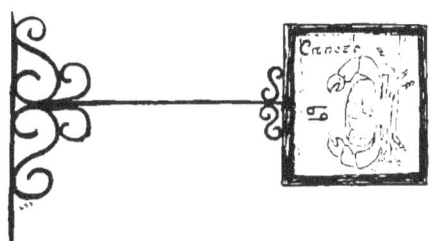

2. Tree Day.
 Ninety-Three's LEGENDA comes out. Ye gods and little fishes!!
3. Professor on her way to consult a physician about her alarming insomnia, falls asleep in the Boston street car, and does not awake until car stops at terminus of line.
4. Dr. Alexander McKenzie, of Cambridge, preaches in the Chapel.
6. Exams. begin.
9. Old gentleman visiting Art Building: "There, Sarey, that's Apollo; and this here's Apollinaris, his wife."
10. Float.
11. G. B. Willcox, of Chicago Theological Seminary, preaches in the Chapel.
15. Last day of exams.
 Hymn 608 given out in Chapel.

> "In vain I task my aching brain,
>   In vain the sage's thoughts I scan;
> I only feel how weak I am,
>   How poor and blind is man.
> And now my spirit sighs for home,
>   And longs for sight whereby to see."

16. Senior Day.
20. Commencement.
21. Exodus.

22. One of our editors in earnest conversation with sister who expects to enter college as Freshman in September: "When you come to college there will be some class secrets you cannot tell even to your sister. For instance, when we go back in September, '94 is going to appear in caps and gowns. *That's* something which you should not tell your sister."

7. Academic year begins 8 A. M., September 7th.
   Arrival of '97.
   Preliminary instructions to Freshmen.
   I. Write home to mamma.
   II. Tell us all about "our class" in the High School.
   III. Make yourself perfectly at home in the Faculty parlor and Society Hall.
   IV. Decide which of the societies you will join.
   V. Be sure to take the teacher's place at dinner. If that is not attainable, take the opposite's.
   VI. Go into the elevator as soon as the door is opened, so as not to keep the Faculty waiting for you.
8. Little '97 is introduced to domestic work.
9. Overheard in the bookstore: "Will you please give me everything a Freshman needs?"
10. Dr. Randolph McKinn, of Washington, preaches in the Chapel.
12. Dignity drapes itself in black.
14. Sophomore Reception.
    Secretary to Board of Examiners as new member of the Faculty is presented: "Oh! there is no need of an introduction; I know all the Freshmen."
15. A few (?) requests for change of elective presented to the Council.
17. Prof. W. H. Ryder, of Andover, preaches in the Chapel.
18. Miss ——, '97, consults professor as to advisability of keeping up Greek, in view of her joining a Greek Letter Society.

19. Head of College Hall at close of lecture on Rules and Regulations: "Young ladies, this ten o'clock rule is no *light* matter."
23. Third anniversary of the first and only absence from recitation of Anna Theodora Skidmore, '94.
24. Dr. A. H. Quint, of Boston, preaches in the Chapel.
29. Instructor in Junior Rhetoric: "What are they digging that trench for?" Professor of Philosophy: "Perhaps to put the Juniors in after they have ended their *brief* course." Instructor in Rhetoric: "Oh, no! It's too deep for them."
30. In German class, Freshman translating: "I am to-day into the city been." Instructor: "But that is not right, Miss ——." Freshman: "Oh, yes it is! I looked up every word in the dictionary, and have them all written down here in my book."

3. Sophomore could not perform her Chemistry experiment, as she had been unable to find the H_2O.
7. Ninety-Four's class history: "The Taming of the Shrew," after Shakespeare (a long way after).
11. Section-books appear.
13. Tennis association dissolves.

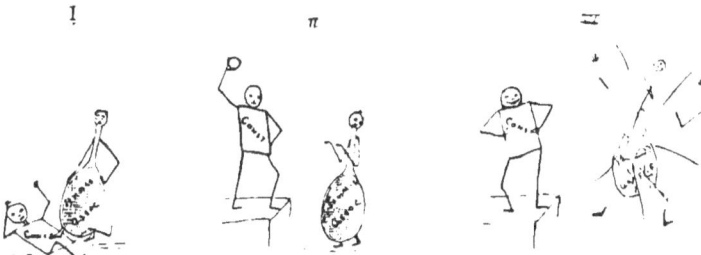

14. Class elections.

"But, children, you should never let
Your angry passions rise;
Your little hands were never made
To tear each other's eyes.

Let dogs delight to bark and bite,
For 'tis their nature to;
Let bears and lions growl and fight,
For God hath made them so."
—*Isaac Watts.*

15. Rev. J. H. Ecob preaches in the Chapel.
16. Lecture by Mr. Clark.
18. Office hours for College Settlement dues.   Freshman comes to pay her laundry bill.
21. Lecture by Miss Stebbins in the Chapel.
22. Prof. W. N. Rice preaches in the Chapel.
25. Lecture by Mr. Clark.
26. Psychological monstrosity incident.
30. Lecture by Mr. Clark.
31. All Halloween.

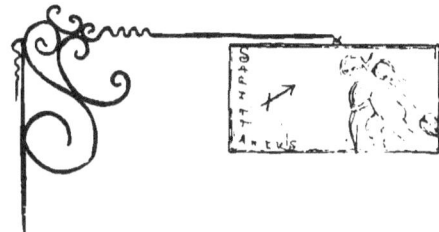

1. Announcement that '97 will raise $1,250 for the athletic field before Christmas.
4. Mrs. Claflin reads to Seniors " Reminiscences of Whittier."
5. Rev. P. S. Moxom preaches in the Chapel.
6. Ninety-Seven's basket-ball nine organized.
7. Election Day.
   Instructor in Senior Bible: One of the first things about Zarathustrianism is that they believed in a constant advance toward an ideal state of protection."
   (Note: The instructor is a Republican.)
10. Prince Wolkonsky.
    Students give three cheers for Prince ——?
12. Rev. J. W. Bixler, of New London, Conn., preaches in the Chapel.
15. Lecture by Mr. Horace Scudder.
    We talk woman's rights.
16. Dr. McKenzie talks to students.
    Professor of Elocution, illustrating: " And this is the gesture one uses when she says, 'Oh! I've had a good dinner!' But you'll not use it very often."
19. Dr. Walcott Calkins preaches in the Chapel.
21. Forty-four Seniors and forty-five Juniors have unexcused absences from Chapel.
26. Rev. A. S. Fuller preaches in the Chapel.
27. Professor Goodale.
30. Thanksgiving.
    Things we are thankful for:—
       The advertisements.
       That we do not have beef more than fourteen times a week on an average.
       That there are still one or two members of '94 who are not chronic invalids.

1. Senior: "I don't see how Harriet Martineau ever got her hair up that way; do you?"
   Freshman: "I'm afraid I don't know her. I know a good many girls by sight, whose names I haven't learned yet."
3. Dr. D. Merriman preaches in the Chapel.
4. Ground broken for athletic field.
9. Ninety-Four receives the Faculty.
   Another run on excuse blanks.
   On account of '94's good record, the privilege of registering for absence from college is extended to '95.
10. Dr. J. L. Hurlburt preaches in the Chapel.
    Miss Atwood, Chairman of Christian Association of Smith College, speaks in the Chapel.
11. Reception for Mr. and Mrs. Gilder.
12. One hundred and thirty dollars and fifty cents have been *already* raised by '97 for the athletic field.
13. "If any one shall be so unfortunate as to be exposed to any contagious disease during the vacation, will she communicate with the physician of the College before she returns."

  4. We all register before 8 a. m. If not, why not?
 10. Exams. begin again.
 14-20. Illness of President Shafer.
 20. Death of President Shafer.
 22. Funeral service.
 25. Day of Prayer.
 31. Recitations resumed.

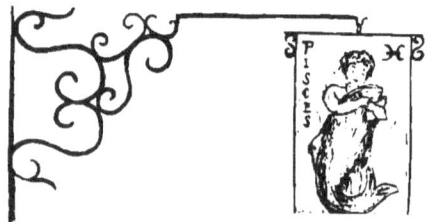

2. H₂S in Chemistry 1, and boiled codheads in Zoölogy.
5. Snow fight between '96 and '97.*
6. Black eyes and court-plaster.
7. Class in Zoölogy attend lecture in Boston. Gentleman in railroad station, seeing professor expounding theory of evolution to crowd of girls, inquires whether she is a patent medicine woman or an evangelist.
10. Contribution received by Legenda Board. "Stupidity of E. B. S.," fully illustrated by the author.
12. Dr. H. H. Furness, from Philadelphia, reads from "As You Like It."
14. St. Valentine's Day.

The Valentines We Write.

These violets, inasmuch as they partake of the nature of not-Being, which must, as the bond of not-Being, have the Being of the not-Being, just as Being must have as a bond the not-Being of not-Being in order to perfect its own Being, must also partake of the nature of the understanding of

THE CLASS IN PHILOSOPHY X.

in regard to the nature of Being and

* See page 200.

not-Being; that is, of the perfection of not-Being. But, inasmuch as they partake of the nature of Being, they partake of the nature of the Being of the Being, and of the not-Being of the not-Being, and so must also partake of the nature of that true wisdom which regards

OUR PROFESSOR

with a love and reverence which is eternal, underived, ever abiding, unchangeable.

19. Class photographer to one of the twins: "Why! you've already had one sitting this morning."
20. Ninety-Six votes to keep the rules.
21. Head of house reports not a single light up after ten last night.
22. "We're going to have a birthday celebration at our table to-night." Absent-minded Senior: "Why! Whose birthday is it?"
25. Bishop C. B. Galloway preaches.
26. Mrs. Susan S. Fessenden speaks in Chapel.

Agitation prevails in the Magazine Board for fear its picture will not appear in the LEGENDA.

27. Calmness restored.

1. Eight hundred people remark that "March comes in like a lamb."
3. Junior Social for Freshmen.
   LEGENDA Board holds a meeting at Rehearsal.
5. Constitution of Tennis Association exhumed from "Catacombs."
6. "Birdie" cuts chapel. Excuse, "Prevented by an angel."
10. Ninety-Seven elects her Freshman president. Little dears heart-broken because no one tried to haze them.
11. Reading by Professor Palmer in Stone Hall parlor.
    The fire is lighted.
12. Head of house reading notice: "Thirty per cent off if twenty-five go; sixty per cent off if fifty go; one hundred and thirty-five per cent off if more than seventy-five go!!!
13. Freshmen announce to College at large their candidates for Tree Day officers.
15. Ninety-Four has a quorum.
16. Art Society moves into its new hall.
17. Freshman: "The Agora is going to have an open meeting to-night, and they've invited *lots* of Freshmen. Isn't it nice of them?"
21. Beginning of '94's last vacation.
31. One of our editors to Editor in Chief: "Well, there's *one* bright thing in the LEGENDA that I didn't originate."

NAMES	Tues. Mar. 6	Wed. Mar. 7	Thurs. Mar. 8	Fri. Mar. 9	Sat. Mar. 10	Sun. Mar. 11	Tues. Mar. 13	Wed. Mar. 14	Thurs. Mar. 15	Fri. Mar. 16	Sat. Mar. 17	Sun. Mar. 18
Professor of Botany.	u	a	u	u	u	a	u	a	a	u	1	a
Associate Professor of Botany.	1	a	a	a	a	a	a	a	a	a	u	a
Professor of Chemistry.	u	u	a	u	u	1	u	a	a	a	a	a
Professor of Elocution.	a	a	u	u	a	u	u	u	a	a	a	a
Professor of French.	a	a	1	a	1	u	a	a	a	a	a	a
Professor of German.	a	a	a	a	a	1	a	a	a	a	a	u
Professor of Geology.	a	a	a	a	a	a	a	a	a	a	a	a
Professor of Greek [1]	a	u	u	a	a	1	a	a	a	a	a	a
Professor of Greek [2]	a	a	u	a	a	a	a	a	a	a	a	a
Professor of Hebrew.	1	u	1	a	a	a	1	a	1	a	a	a
Professor of History.	a	a	a	a	a	a	a	a	a	a	u	a
Associate Professor of History [1]	a	u	1	a	1	1	a	a	a	a	a	a
Associate Professor of History [2]	a	1	a	a	a	a	1	1	a	u	a	a
Professor of History of Art.	u	a	a	a	a	a	a	a	a	a	a	a

NAMES.	Tues Mar 6	Wed Mar	Thurs Mar 8	Fri Mar 9	Sat Mar 10	Sun May 11	Tues Mar 13	Wed Mar 14	Thurs Mar	Fri Mar 16	Sat Mar 17	Sun Mar 18
Professor of Latin	/	/	/	/	/	a	/	/	/	/	/	/
Professor of Literature	u	u	u	u	a	a	u	u	/	u	u	a
Professor of Mathematics	a	a	a	a	a	a	a	a	a	a	a	a
Associate Professor of Mathematics	a	u	u	a	a	a	/	a	u	/	u	a
Associate Professor of Mathematics (2)	a	a	/	u	a	a	/	u	/	u	a	a
Professor of Philology	a	a	a	a	a	a	a	a	a	a	a
Professor of Philosophy	u	a	a	a	a	/	a	a	a	a	/
Professor of Physics	a	/	a	a	/	/	/	/	a	/	/	/
Professor of Rhetoric	/	/	u	/	/	a	/	/	/	/	/	/
Professor of Zoology	a	u	a	a	/	a	a	a	a	a	a

April 16.   LEGENDA goes to print.
 Board reduced to splinters.

All the Time.

Monday	Green bananas.
Tuesday	Half bananas.
Wednesday	Bananas sliced.
Thursday	Bananas and oranges.
Friday	Banana fritters.
Saturday	Banana ice cream.
Sunday	Banana jelly.

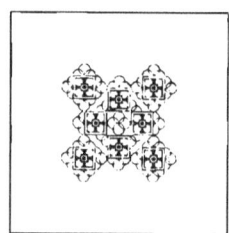

College Views

Pictorial and Literary.

Ninety-Four.

THERE'S no limit to the knowledge she has picked up here at College.
You may look through many ages, and inquire of all the sages,
Seek the learning that was burning in their mighty brains; then, turning,
    Go to '94 for answer to your questions hard.

Ask it if you will in Spanish, French, Italian, Greek, or Danish;
She may answer you in Sanscrit, Hebrew, Latin, all of it,
Or she'll sprechen it in Dutch; it won't matter very much,
    For she's the infant prodigy now grown to high estate.

She is posted on theology, and zoölogy, and psychology;
Had a course in philology, embriology and geology,
And in all the other ologies; taught in all the other colleges
    On this or on the other side of any ocean.

She can manage a micrometer, dynometer, or photometer;
Measure lens by a spherometer, and the air by a barometer;
Measure wind by anemometer, set in place a cathetometer,
    Or use any instrument you may devise.

She'll elucidate mathematics; hydrostatics, or pneumatics;
Show she's versed in neumismatics, or the laws of social statics.
She'll discuss all things aquatic, though erratic, quite emphatic;
    That she knows a thing or two you must admit.

All the men of ancient times, down from Adam to old Grimes,
Polycarp and Alexander, Sophocles, Anaximander,
Dido and Democritus, Solon and Theocritus,
Thucydides, Euripedes, Thales and Diogenes,
Theodosius and Eustachius, Epictetus, Aristarchus,
Euclid, Anaxagoras, Aristotle, and Pythagoras,
    You will fail to find a name she doesn't know.

She can name to you the wars, give result, events, and cause;
First the contest with the Devil, international, then civil.
She will tell the name and date, give the leaders and their fate,
    Or any other facts that you may care to know.

She'll describe the latest station that's acquired by any nation,
Be they Goths, or Franks, or Vandals,—them she knows even to their sandals;
Aztecs, Peruvians, and Mexicans, Scandinavians, Russians, Texans,
    Do they live in present ages or in prehistoric time.

Music, politics, and art, may be conversation's part,
Or it may be Browning's sonnets, or the very latest bonnets,
Poets, authors, and the fashion; anything that you may chance on,
    She can talk and talk and talk until you're tired.

THERE has recently been discovered a fragment of a dialogue, which seems undoubtedly Platonic. Some eminent scholars, it is true, have questioned the genuineness of the fragment, on the ground that the external evidence is far from convincing. These have not given due importance to the internal evidence,—which to us seems so clear as to leave no shadow of doubt as to the authenticity of the Weno. The style all through bears a close resemblance to that of certain admittedly Platonic writings. In places we are strongly reminded of the Phaedrus and of the Theaetetus. There are also suggestions of the Republic. We should be inclined to place the Weno in the later and more mature period of Plato's writing,—for he has seemed to gather up all that was best and finest in the styles of each one in this dialogue.

The Weno.

SOCRATES: "My dear Weno, whence come you, and whither are you going?"

WENO: "I am come from Stratonicus, Socrates, and I am going to take a walk outside the wall, for I have been in his paroikodomema[1] since Kalia hiera,[2] which is a long while, and our friend Lege, O Anthrope,[3] advises me to walk in the country. Come with me; let us go to Tupelo, and sit at some quiet spot and continue the subject on which we were conversing."

SOCRATES: "Yes, let us continue the conversation; but do not let us go to the point you mention, for I am a lover of knowledge, and the men who live in the city are my teachers,

[1] παροικοδομημα.   [2] καλα ὁρα.   [3] λεγε, ὠ ανθρωπε.

and not the trees and the country. Let us rather go to the bibliotheke,[4] the general gathering place."

WENO: "Certainly, Socrates, if you wish; but why not to the arche[5] of the angaron, may I ask?"

SOCRATES: "Merely because there are no chairs in he tore angaron arche. If in he bibliotheke any question of history, ethics, or science should arise, Godfreippus and Pierkites are ready to answer it for us."

WENO: "Very true; I had not thought of that."

SOCRATES: "Well, now, having arrived I will sit down, and you had better do so likewise, and choose any posture in which you will be most comfortable. To return, then, to our discussion, you consider your State the perfect one?"

WENO: "Yes, Socrates."

SOCRATES: "Then relate to me the composition."

WENO: "Certainly. I have told you how the State was increasing constantly; now it is our design that the State may increase to any limit which is consistent with unity; that is the limit."

SOCRATES: "Yes; that is excellent. But the larger the State grows the more time, and art, and skill will be needed by the guardians; who, as we said before, must be the older, the wiser, and the more reasonable in order to rule wisely over the younger, the more ignorant and the more foolish?"

WENO: "Surely, Socrates; and to aid in this, there is a wise provision in the State which exists not elsewhere."

SOCRATES: "What is that, Weno?"

WENO: "You know, Socrates, that each one of the subjects has something to do in the State. Now of these subjects the wisest, the bravest, and the most patient are selected, and each guardian has one."

SOCRATES: "What are these attendants called, Weno?"

WENO: "Hitherto they have been known as "domestic girls"; but, Jewettacus, one of the guardians objects seriously to the term."

SOCRATES: "But can she suggest a better?"

WENO: "No, Socrates, she cannot; but you might."

SOCRATES: "Well, then, let them be called guardian angels, for that expresses both what they are and what they need to be. But in a State so rapidly increasing there must be many more subjects than are needed for this purpose. Did you not say that each one has something to do in the State?"

WENO: "Yes, Socrates, certainly. All subjects within the limits aid in the lighter manual labor, or in the clerical work of the offices, libraries, and departments of instruction. Much valuable information and discipline are thus secured to the subjects, though the time occupied is never more than one periodos[6] daily."

SOCRATES: "Indeed, Weno, there is much wisdom in this provision. I see clearly that it must greatly lessen the number of mercenaries and slaves necessary for the administration of a State, and so indirectly increase the revenues. But has it not its disadvantages?"

WENO: "I think not, Socrates."

SOCRATES: "I should like, if I may, to ask a few questions, Weno."

WENO: "Certainly, Socrates. I will try to answer discreetly, and if I make mistakes you will be sure to correct me."

SOCRATES: "Do all the subjects perform this duty willingly?"

WENO: "It must be confessed, Socrates, that many do not."

SOCRATES: "To such, then, the labor is compulsory?"

WENO: "Yes."

SOCRATES: "But it would seem, then, that the work would not always be performed to the satisfaction of the State."

WENO: "Your objections shows great discernment, Socrates. But to avoid this difficulty there are special officers appointed, and they in their turn select subordinates,—supervisors, called hegemones,[7]— so that no work can with impunity be neglected."

SOCRATES: "That, too, is a beneficent provision, Weno. But this effect upon the moral nature of the subjects should certainly be considered, since it is more important than the performance of outward duties."

WENO: "Yes, Socrates; but do you not see that the influence of this work, rendered heartily, is invaluable in producing during the years of mental training habits of accuracy, self-reliance, and genuine sympathy with all workers?"

SOCRATES: "No doubt you are right, Weno. But have you not said that the service is in many cases not rendered heartily?"

WENO: "Yes."

SOCRATES: "If that is so, must there not be frequent unpleasantness between the subjects and the officers you mention?"

WENO: "That is true."

SOCRATES: "And the soul of the guardian is full of spirit, is it not?"

WENO: "Yes, Socrates."

SOCRATES: "But these spirited natures, although they have the advantage of being unaffected by any danger, even by that of going up to the lophon* after dark, are apt to be furious with everybody who opposes them?"

WENO: "Very true, Socrates."

SOCRATES: "And all come to fear them when they are angry?"

WENO: "Most true."

SOCRATES: "Then do you not see where that leads you, Weno? Can the best work be done by a subject when he is fearful?"

WENO: "Certainly not, Socrates. But then, the subject becomes accustomed to the wrath of his guardian, and in any given case merely does what Homer in the Odyssee represents Odysseus as doing in the words,

'He beat his breast, and thus reproached his heart.
Endure, O heart; far worse hast thou endured,
And wilt endure.'

And therefore this difficulty which seemed so great, turns out to be none at all, but an advantage; for thereby is much control taught to the youth, than which nothing is more useful."

SOCRATES: "What you say is true, Weno, but it suggests to me another question I should like to ask."

WENO: "Proceed, Socrates."

SOCRATES: "I will. Tell me, Weno, do not the subjects sometimes try to evade and circumvent their supervisors?"

WENO: "I cannot deny that, Socrates."

SOCRATES: "Then, Weno, you must admit that the subject will become keen and shrewd; that he will learn how to flatter his superior officer in word, and to indulge himself in deed; that his soul will become small and unrighteous. Dangers and fears which are too much for his truth and honesty will come upon him in early years, when the tenderness of youth is unequal to them, and he will be driven into crooked ways. From the first he will practice deception and retaliation, and he must become stunted and warped. Can you deny, Weno, that such will be the result of the system?"

WENO: "It is proven, abundantly proven, Socrates."

SOCRATES: "And there are many more proofs that this system is a pernicious one, which, if you would like, we can discuss."

WENO: "No, Socrates, I am fully convinced; and if you could only persuade everybody, as you do me, of the truth of your words, there would be more peace and fewer evils among us."

* The Tower.

Editorial Trials.

WHILE awaiting the distribution of the mail, a LEGENDA editor stops to talk to a Freshman, as befits a good society member.

FRESHMAN: "Oh! you're on the LEGENDA, aren't you? I'm going to buy one this year."

EDITOR (smilingly): "That's very gratifying. I am sure. What has thus early convinced you of the merits of the LEGENDA?"

FRESHMAN: "Well, my roommate will not have her picture taken for me. But she is on the Banjo Club; so her picture will be in the LEGENDA, and I'll get it that way."

EDITOR (somewhat crestfallen): "That is not a great compliment to the editors."

FRESHMAN: "Oh, well! I haven't known you long enough to want *your* picture yet."

The editor disappears into the mob at the post-office door, silently meditating on the advisability of advertising the LEGENDA as a picture book to amuse Freshmen and other infants.

Another Dialogue.

THE Editor in Chief of the *Wellesley Magazine*, too full of indignation to contain herself, confides her feelings to the girl who happens to be walking along the corridor beside her.

EDITOR: "I cannot understand how anyone can think a man like Mr. —— able to take the direction of a great publication like the —— *Magazine!*"

FRESHMAN (warmly): "I'm sure I quite agree with you. He is just about suited to the *Wellesley Magazine!*"

The editor resolves henceforth to confine her criticisms to the sanctum of the Magazine board.

Patent Library Cap.

DESIGNED especially for the use of students in the Library. The visor screens the eyes from the electric lights; the padded ear-pieces prevent injury to ear drums from the noise; the cape at the back protects from draughts; the electric light at the top, connected with a pocket battery, is useful in the dark alcoves. This cap is also adapted to underground exploration, and will be of value to those who visit the Catacombs. Being made in the class colors, it will aid the factotums in identifying those needed for their quorums.

Originality.

THE present demand for originality is abominable. No one but a genius can live comfortably; and if an ordinary mortal is deluded into thinking that it is a just demand, he cannot walk, or eat, or sleep, or perform any of the ordinary functions of life, without a guilty feeling that he is plodding along in a beaten track. Does he chance to meet a friend, he withholds the pleasant word of greeting for fear of saying something commonplace. Does he see some object of beauty in his daily walk, he is compelled to refrain from describing it for lack of novel phrases. Dubbed a plagiarist if he presumes to express himself naturally, he sneaks through his existence, and continually sighs because he was not born in primeval times, when all thoughts were original.

A Riddle.

THE room is crowded with Philosophy students, who are awaiting the coming of the Professor, at whose shrine of learning they mentally bow down in adoration. They are all enthusiastic in the subject, and, with one accord, emphatically declare its ascendency over every other study. Zealously they discuss the question for the approaching hour. But a messenger brings word that the lesson for the day must be suspended, on account of the illness of the Professor. Tell me, ye Wise, why do the faces of the students beam with joy?

A Modern Improvement.

IN the days sung by old Homer,
When Odysseus was a roamer,
Eos used to come and waken
    Weary mortals from their sleep.
But in Wellesley she's not lingered,—
Morn's fair daughter "rosy-fingered."—
For the girl her task hath taken
    Who the corridor doth sweep!

A VIEW IN THE LIBRARY.

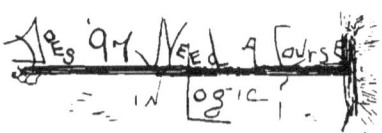

SCENE . . . Second floor center.
TIME . . . Eight-thirty A. M.

Head of Domestic Department stands gazing at Delinquent Freshman, who holds broom and pan of dust in her hand. A hymn is heard from the distant Chapel.

H. OF D. D. (severely): "Don't you know you ought not to be doing this work now?"
D. F. (humbly): "Yes'm; but isn't this better than not doing it at all?"
H. OF D. D. (still severely): "That matter must rest with your own conscience."
D. F. (earnestly): "Don't you see,—no one but me will ever suffer if I don't go to Chapel; and think how many people would be inconvenienced by all this dust!"
H. OF D. D. leans against the wall for support, while D. F. carries her dust to the dust-shaft,—and a passing Senior smiles behind the sleeve of her gown.

Their Melancholy Mien.

Three girls from vacation the railway took;
Each entered the car with saddened look,
And seeking out a retired nook,
Awaited the Wellesley call.

A bright little maiden of four or more
Watched from her corner of minutes a score;
Then softly let fall into father's ear
The question, "Why are so many here?"

"Hush, little daughter," he gently said,
As he turned on his shoulder her curly head;
"If 'tis a funeral, as I take it to be,
'Tis a sorrowful day for all the three."

— *Wellesley Prelude.*

The Requirements for a Class Treasurer.

CLEAR, level head; precision and exactness developed by a rigorous course of mathematical training; the entire absence of sensitiveness; an unlimited store of patience and perseverance; a faith in the generosity of mankind that nothing can shake; above all, a cheerful countenance.

"O riddle me riddle," the schoolboy said;
"O tell me, thou maid with blue eyes,
The difference between the Wellesley thou lovest,
And the great gates of Paradise."

"I can riddle your riddle," the Freshman replied;
"A difference in patrons is all;
St. Peter is guardian of Heaven's gate,
While Wellesley's gate keeper is Paul."

Theme No. 32.

RUBBED my eyes in bewilderment and gazed around me. A bent, emaciated figure crouched in the shadow of my lamp, and gave forth from time to time the most heartrending sighs. "Speak!" I gasped. "What are you? Why are you here? Speak." With a groan he turned and faced me, and I saw a little old man, bent almost double; his face was wan, and in his eyes was a look of unsatisfied longing that pierced the heart. Then in a sepulchral voice he whispered: "I am the ghost of the idea for the thirty-second theme. Pity me!" and vanished.

Boat Song.

The dark o' the night was comin' fast,
For 'twas avenin', afther tay was past,
An' jist the time whin boatin's swate,
An' gals come down all dressed so nate,
    Bay jabbers.

The Cap'ns were followin' after the rist,
A-runnin' down hill like all possist,
An' like an old tin fish horn rung
The accints of the Freshmen tongue,
    Bay jabbers.

The Sophs are a-watchin' 'em up on the shore;
First up goes one, thin another oar,
Boats goin' this way, thin goin' that,
An' now one crayture's lost her hat,
    Bay jabbers!

" Pick up that hat," the Cap'n said,
" An' jam it quick on the top o' yer head;
For the way is long, and the lake is wide,
An' the boats must be hauled up side by side,"
    Bay jabbers.

Steer shy o' that sailboat out on the lake,
Or your tayther'll be telegraphed to a wake.
That's Hunnewell's boat; there's a man inside,
An' ye must kape up the College pride,
    Bay jabbers.

" Wait a bit, now," says one, " and rist,
For the dress I have on is me very bist,
An' the boat has a lake, an' the wather's high,
An' I'll jist haul it up to kape it dry."
    Bay jabbers.

The bell is ringin'f or half past siven;
From six till thin is the time that's given;
An' they'll have to row at an awful rate
To be at the hall at a quarther of eight,
    Bay jabbers!

But with all their rowin' they don't get in;
So jist to punish thim for their sin
They lock thim out of the beautiful gate,
Cos they're not in at a quarther of eight,
    Bay jabbers.

So they sit thim down on the cold stone steps,
As if they were nothin' but common Preps;
And nobody comes to let thim in,
But lave thim there to repint of their sin;
    Bay jabbers!

An Incident.

SCENE . . . . A Wellesley class room.
DRAMATIS PERSONÆ . . Professor of Philosophy.
                       Class of Students.
TIME . . . . Two minutes after the lunch bell.

PROFESSOR LOQUITUR.

OW, to recapitulate, if opinion is purely individual, there is no possibility of error. For instance, if you should look up and see a blue horse with a red tail, green teeth and purple eyes, come in at the door, there would actually be such a horse there for you."

Class glances involuntarily at door. Door opens. Enter Professor of Physics, gazes at class, and retires in confusion. Professor continues her remarks; these, however, are lost on the class.

The College pin they did talk o'er,
When a Senior raised one question more:
"Why don't the Faculty have one, too?
The letter F for them would do."

The Junior slowly shook her head;
"There might come times," she gently said—
"April first would be one, you know—
When they might not like to go labeled so."

— *Wellesley Prelude.*

The Lament of the Unathletic Maiden.

I'M born a century late,
    And I'm utterly out of my sphere;
My ideas are all out of date,
    And so are my talents, I fear.

I used to play tennis, and row,
    Or walk for an hour with a friend;
But now all my pleasures must go,
    All my simple delights have an end.

'Tis only the crews that may row,
    And I,— I belong to no crew;
My methods in tennis are slow,
    And not scientific or new.

Now, basket-ball looks very nice,
    But then I am not on the team;
And to play golf I must pay the price
    Of joining *that* club, it would seem.

But walking,— it surely remains!
    No, there's the pedestrian band,
That wanders all over the plains,
    And climbs all the hills in the land.

And what's a poor maiden to do
    Who isn't athletic at all,
Who's no time to row on a crew,
    Or learn scientific baseball?

No time, since she has a desire
    To do some *brain* work now and then;
And, somehow, her lessons require
    A minute or two spent on *them*.

It seems there is nothing to do
    But give up all ideas of fun,
And exercise watching the crew,
    Or seeing some brilliant home run.

The Stuff that Dreams are Made Of.

IT was a weird night—a night for ghosts to be abroad. The storm played a wild symphony through the shivering woods; the snow, driven by the reckless wind, whirled in blinding masses, making the atmosphere white. Half waking from a deep sleep, I became conscious of a presence in my room,—a presence which seemed to bring with it the chill of the storm without. Gradually it approached my bed, until it bent over me, whispering: "What were the causes for the failure of constitutional government under the House of Lancaster? If a man can throw a cricket ball fifty yards vertically upward, how far can he throw it on a horizontal plane? What is the essential difference between the poetry of Milton and that of Spenser? Wherein is Zarathustrianism a higher form of religion than Buddhism? What—" I heard no more. When I next became conscious of life, the sun was shining on the fallen snow, and it was the day after to-morrow.

Triolet.

I'VE a cold in my head;
    I snuffle and sneeze;
My smell-sense has fled;
I've a cold in my head.
My eyes are all red;
    My voice is a wheeze;
I've a cold in my head;
    I snuffle and sneeze.

"A Word to the Wise."

THE Senior Wardrobe is not a convenience for Freshmen. From various recent occurrences it is to be feared that this is not distinctly understood. It is doubtless very pleasant for the Freshmen — to find a resting place for their wraps in a location more available than the regions commonly known as the "Catacombs." But it is not so agreeable for those members of the College community who have been taught through three long years to regard the article of furniture in question as sacred to the mysterious something known as "Senior Dignity." Therefore we would respectfully recommend that a notice to this effect be placed in a conspicuous position on the Freshman bulletin board, and that the Class of '07 be requested to consult the same immediately.

Wed to Elocution.

WRITTEN IN SOPHIC PENT IETRA ANIMATI'N.

To do thee justice, is the tongue
Not made for speech, in ardor wrung,
And yearns expression e'en in empty thought.

Ah, cruel! as with rythm deep
I breathe, I hold, give out, in sweep
Of sound intent, the glowing voice is caught
In faltering elements; then quick
Before faint eyes there dances thick
A myriad blue stars,—powers that hold
Conditions of our rise and fall;
    And now I fall.

But stop! that fall
Starts from the center, and the members fold
Upon themselves,— examples of the wise
Progression of the trained, unconscious mind;
And, paradox—in falling do I rise,
And through my *opposition*, grace I find.

— M. H., '06.

A Lament.

NOT so many months ago, when June breezes ceased to blow,
   I had friends,—live friends, in truth, a friendship rare ;
Now no August heat doth blight, but that friendship's vanished quite.
   Why ? They've come from great Chicago and the Fair !

      Oh, communion once was bliss ! Who would then have thought that this
         Would encounter greater strain than it could bear?
      Once I hung on every word,—that was long before I heard
         What they'd seen in great Chicago, at the Fair !

            Once I ever longed to know of their goings to and fro ;
               Who would then have thought that now I shouldn't care,—
            Shouldn't care for anything ! O the changes time will bring
               When 'tis spent in great Chicago, at the Fair !

An Agnostic.

DON'T care whether Bougainvillia is gymnoblastic or calyptoblastic, nor why the second derivative of space with respect to time represents acceleration, nor how William Rufus influenced the development of English institutions, nor what Buddhism teaches of the nature of a sentient being, nor what a fringe of consciousness is. I don't want to know anything.

An Attempt at Catalectic Verse.

ONE awesome night at half-past twelve,
   At center of Fifth Floor,
The grisly shape which haunts that place,
   Once, by myself, I saw.

And thus it moaned: "I am, alas!
   The ghost of a pickled cat:
My home was once in Natick town,
   I hunted mouse and rat;

"When one sad day they boxed me up,
   And sent to Wellesley,
Where my ninth precious life was ta'en
   To serve Zoölogy.

"Much of myself is gone: the rest
   All pickled here you spy,
And on Examination night
   Alone set free am I.

"Then, wandering forth for one brief while,
   The murderous maids to see,
I spare them not who spared me not
   For cruel Zoölogy!

"And dance and yowl around the beds
   Whereon my murderers lie;
And then I wis they rue the day,
   On which they made me die."

Vivisection.

FROM THE WELLESLEY PRELUDE.

If vivisection merely
   Afflicted dogs, and such,
Although it would be shocking,
   It wouldn't hurt so much
As when a human "cœur" is rent
   In twain by human touch.
I pray you, then, have mercy
   On me, a lover true,
Whose heart, in bleeding sections,
   Is carried off by you.

L... '92.

A Sample of a Freshman Class Meeting.

THE other morning the Freshmen remained after chapel for a class meeting. The chairman rose and announced: "I have an invitation for you from the Juniors. They are going to give a social for us next Saturday afternoon. Now, be sure to come, all of you!" Whereupon the chairman sat down again, and the members of the class made a unanimous rush for the door.

Happy children! Roberts has not yet subjected them to his stern sway.

My Thoughts.

I HAD some pretty thoughts one day
Go flitting through my brain;
I took my pen and paper up,
Then they were gone again.

They were as bright as butterflies,
That go from flower to flower;
I chased the happy creatures
For quite a half an hour.

But once when I had grasped them,
The beautiful bright things,
I found I'd brushed the color off;
They, too, had powdered wings.

That they are torn and colorless,
My thoughts, I now deplore,
And wish I had them back again,
Just as they were before.

A Self-consoling Soliloquy.

YES, Mr. Ruskin's literary style is truly an enviable one. It is clear and rhythmical. His is the power of giving language a spiritual grace. His habits of thought show delicate shades of consciousness. His thought is excellent; his choice of diction exquisite. I wonder if undivided attention to literary work is the secret of his success. I hope so. There is some comfort in supposing that even one of the giants of literature could not devote himself to expressing excellent thought in perfect form, and at the same time carry on a conscientious study of Mathematics, Philosophy, Hebrew, Political Economy, and German Literature; and assist in household duties, and take an active part in society life, and help in the LEGENDA, and suffer almost hourly interruptions because of social and political duties.

I Wonder, Don't You?

If girls who talked on concert night
   To guests in hall,
Could only hear how very like
   A clarion call
Sounded their sweetness in
   The ears of all,
I wonder if 'twere possible
   They'd talk at all.
     Don't you?

Wellesley Prelude.

A Valentine.

O Love, the glory of thy being's essence
   Hath shined upon me wondrous bright.
The "isness-of-the-as-it-were" is filling
   My soul with light.
Across the threshold of my consciousness
Hath passed the percept of thy loveliness.

Time, space, what are they to the soul that loveth?
   I blow them from me with a breath!
An *a priori* oneness hath united
   Our souls till death.
Though thou art far, our spirits meet and kiss
In transcendental and eternal bliss.

ON A WINDY DAY.

Office Hours for Countersigning Excuses.

"PLEASE sign my excuses," the Freshman said,
   As she laid them down in a row;
"The reason I didn't come back on time,
   Is because I forgot to, you know."

A Lie.

The Law of Compensation.

A DISTRESSED-LOOKING maiden stood before the dread tribunal of the Domestic Department at College Hall. She pleaded guilty to the crime of forgetting two days in succession the substitute work she had promised to do. It would probably go hard with her, for it was not her first offense, and she trembled as the judge pronounced her fate.

"Well, Caroline, you are not very reliable, are you?"

"No'm; I'm afraid not" (very meekly).

"I think, Caroline, in the future when girls ask you to do their work, you may say that I wish them to get some one else. It will not be best for you to substitute any more."

"I suppose you are right," was the submissive reply; and she turned and passed through the corridors where hard-working, conscientious girls were sweeping for their friends, and she thought of the happy Thanksgiving recess which was coming.

    Life is a grind,
      Work is a flunk;
    You think, think, think,
      And you get nothing thunk.

Before and After.

SHE sat for hours and labored and thought;
    She scribbled, and scratched, and erased;
She counted her words and averaged per cents,
    And endeavored to write with taste.

She finished, at last, with a sigh of relief,
    And legibly copied it all.
She strove to make punctuation correct,
    Nor in worn-out diction to fall.

And then she laid it, with trembling and fear,
    On the altar of Rhetoric stern;
And waited and hoped for a weary week
    For the child of her brain to return.

It came at last, but with tear-dimmed eyes
    She scanned its familiar face.
Was it *this* that had been her joy and pride,
    That had seemed so full of grace?

The glaring letters compelled her gaze;
    "Avoid" and "remodel" they said;
"Felicitous choice"—and a question mark—
    After "unsatisfactory," she read.

She gazed about her in blank despair,
    Then desperately seized her pen.
"I must write another ere nine o'clock!"
    And she labored and thought again.

THE CHAIRMAN OF A COMMITTEE BEARS THE
WEIGHT OF RESPONSIBILITY.

FAMILIAR FIGURES.

SIGNS OF THE TIMES.

Sign of Spring: all trespassers chased off the Norumbega lawn.

Sign of a lecture after chapel: Lord's Prayer and one hymn.

Sign of a Freshman class meeting: general flunk.

> I reached the door, my hand I raised,
> But stopped astonished as I gazed;
> For there before my anxious sight
> Fluttered a paper large and white.
>
> This is the legend that it bore
> That caused me sadly to leave the door:
> "Busy! Don't knock, not even you;
> I'm taking a systematic review!"
> —J. B., '96.

Traditional sign of a Senior class meeting: Senior president attends chapel.

Sign of changing the subject: Mention before a '94 Wabanite of a triangle or his Satanic Majesty.

Sign of a flood: Approach of day set for Shakespeare play.

A Page from a History Notebook.

WARS OF THE S'NOSES.

A. CAUSES.
    I. Mediate.
        a. Inherent oppo'on f Sophs & Freshm.
        b. Amb'n f '97 to make herself conspic.
        Explan.—orig. verdancy.
    II. Immed.
        Fact that '96 got there 1st & hung sp. on '97 bull'n bd, tog w. a chall. 1 yd. long.

B. EVENTS.
    Many faces washed.
    Val. chges made.
    Much coldness & some madness ev. on each side.
    Fort taken b. fce (N. B. look up ts pt. in contemp. hists f both sides).
    Gt. cheerg amg spects—who froze s stiff's pokers.

C. RESULTS.
    I. Dir.
        Sev'l bruised noses, 1 vy blk eye (on ts. subj., ref. to contemp hist f Virg.)
        No decsv effd. Both fac'ns cl. victy. (Bal. f evid. on side f '96.)
    II. Indir.
        a. (Look up in someby's else n. bk.)
        b. Gt. extrav. in matter f excuse blks.
        c. Empty class rooms.
        d. Crutch & inval. chr. worn out.
        e. Resid't frmen turned out f hosp'l.
        Qu. E. D. Could a rat-demon strand 'em?

N. B.— Find out what this has to do w. e. subjt.

Is Zeta Alphas' symbol a gravy bowl or a teapot?

No; '95 will not plant any more trees. Ninety-five is sick o' more trees.

The common property of Φ Σ and Z A,—the grip and the piano.

Noted in any LEGENDA Board meeting: "Isn't this too personal?"

"This thing of mine is very bad and incomplete, I know. I wish you'd make suggestions, and I shall be glad to be sat on."

Ghoughknayptoisquesw.

Phthioux chmeighsc chteighmb lfcorps lkowtenlfyrrhusnetz ghoulmgmuightctcaucz, eausp louayghaughwrmpbd rcesghailnsleon.

KEY.

Phonetics . . .	lau*gh*, thou*gh*, *k*nit, sa*y*s, *p*tarmigan, *ch*amois, cli*que*, s*w*ord.
To	*ph*thisic, Sio*ux*.
Make	dra*chm*, w*eigh*, vi*s*count.
Time	*y*a*ch*t, h*eigh*t, dum*b*.
For	hal*f*, G*e*orge, cor*ps*.
Conference . .	wa*l*k, kno*w*ledge, of*ten*, cal*f*, my*rrh*, bu*r*y, deme*s*ne, wal*tz*.
Committees . .	lou*gh*, lou*gh*, ca*l*m, phle*gm*, g*ui*nea, ou*ght*, in*d*ict, b*eau*fin, *cz*ar.
Use	b*eau*ty, ras*p*berry.
Reformed . . .	co*l*onel, qu*ay*, *e*nough, tau*ght*, *w*rap, sem*p*stress, *b*dellium.
Spelling	Wor*ce*ster, hic*cough*, sa*i*d, ki*ln*, i*s*le, w*o*men, a*nxi*ous.

Notes on the Chief Regulations of Wellesley College.

BY A FRESHMAN.

It is understood that, in general, the rules are made for the purpose of being broken; but if on any special occasion — such as your first week in college, your sixteenth birthday anniversary, or the day you receive your first lecture from the head of the house — you should decide to regard the regulations, I have prepared a reliable exegesis of some of the more difficult points, which I now unhesitatingly submit to posterity.

I. *Without permission from the President, students will not join or leave any department of instruction nor attend any courses except those to which they are assigned.* Permission is not required, however, for the department of instruction conducted by the Sophomores, or the course of cultivation by the members of the several societies.

II. *Students will punctually attend all college exercises; viz., prayers, class-room appointments, domestic work, etc.* The word "punctually" admits of various interpretations, according to the context: in connection with prayers, it means during the singing of the third stanza, or later; with recitations, it is usually taken to mean before the end of the period. With domestic work there can be no fixed rule, as the interpretations differ according to the activity of the superintendent; once a week is a good average.

III. *Public literary exercises will be submitted to the approval of the Professors in charge of the departments of Rhetoric and Elocution,* and then changed afterwards to suit yourself.

IV. *At 10 P. M. students will promptly extinguish their lights, retire, and preserve quiet.* "Promptly" is a contracted expression for "after the second visit from the corridor teacher." After "retire," understand the words "to your own rooms or some one's else." "Quiet," in this case, indicates a little more than the usual degree of quiet preserved in the dining room during dinner.

HEALTH DIRECTIONS.

I. *Students should exercise not less than an hour daily in the open air; but regular practice in the Gymnasium may take the place of one half hour of such exercise.* Or exercise in sweeping the corridor may be substituted for both.

II. *Students are warned against irregularity in diet.* The College provides an extremely regular one.

III. *Every study parlor should be provided with a thermometer. A mean temperature of 70° is advised.* In the north rooms the temperature is a good deal meaner.

Ink must be kept in " safety" stands. It is then warranted to be in a state of constant and uniform overflow, so as to reduce all of your gowns to a uniform spottedness. *They may be purchased at the College bookstore,*—at double prices.

Students will not remove these cards from the rooms. If you wish to carry a copy constantly with you, for purposes of reference and study, we advise you to purchase our annotated edition.

Side Talks with Our Girls.

UNDER THIS HEADING WE WILL CHEERFULLY ANSWER ALL REASONABLE QUESTIONS SENT US BY OUR GIRL READERS.—THE EDITORS.

ANXIOUS FRESHMAN AND OTHERS.—Such requests for old examination papers are constantly received at our office. We cannot approve of the unscholarly process usually known as "cramming"; but a systematic review previous to examinations is very helpful, and to aid in such review we gladly publish the following typical questions:—

Mathematics: Supposing the average girl to be 5 ft. 2 in. in length, 3 ft. in breadth (including sleeves), and 1 ft. in depth; how many girls can be contained in the Post Office (10 ft. x 3 ft.) at one time?

History: What is the date of the Reformation?
Ans. Feb. 20, 1894.

Botany: Distinguish between a sycamore and a maple. (See Annals of Class of '95.)

Greek: What is the significance of $\Phi \Sigma$ and $Z \Lambda$? (Consult young woman mentioned in Calendar, September 18th.)

Physics: Calculate pressure to square inch on surface of each individual in the mob at the Chapel door at the moment when the organ stops playing, and amount of force necessary to close doors.

DOLLY.—We do not advise applying for membership in any of the more exclusive associations, but consider you perfectly eligible for either of the triangle societies. You ask for further information concerning them. The merit of the older society is attested by the character of its founder, whose likeness is worn by all its members. The younger is the offspring of Zeta Alpha. The significance of its name is not, as many have supposed, "Dear Things," nor yet "Doll's Tea Party," but has reference to the thought which was in the mind of the charter members when the society was formed, in their Freshman year: "Destined to Zeta Alpha."

UNSOPHISTICATED FRESHMAN.—Yes; it was a mistake for you to offer to pay the College physician for her services.

ANXIOUS INQUIRER.— No, there have not been any mob riots that we know of at the boat-landing. The broken oars, paddles, etc., to which you refer were probably left by friends who borrowed boats without the owners' knowledge, and forgot to mention their mishaps.

FROM THE RURAL DISTRICTS.—Wellesley has not yet established an agricultural department. You evidently refer to the ploughed land between Music Hall and Stone Hall. That is our athletic field.

INJURED SOPHOMORE.—No; we do not think you could bring a breach of promise case against the Junior who used your room as a wardrobe, study, and rendezvous during the whole of last year, and then failed to invite you to join her society. You should have recognized that as an essential part of the process known as "cultivating Freshmen," and should not have built your hopes upon it, since it is not generally considered at all binding. We are sorry for your disappointment. Do not let this experience ruin your life, but learn from it to place your confidence where it is better deserved.

GOLDILOCKS.—My dear child, don't think of meddling with such a dangerous thing as H_2SO_4! If you need a hair wash, try Wellesley College Sweet Pea Lotion. Since the inventor has been so kind as to name his hair restorer in honor of the Class of '95, he should have the patronage of every loyal Wellesley girl.

SWEET SIXTEEN.—No; it is not good form for a Freshman to go to a Junior class meeting.

WEARIED BRAIN WORKER.—For light reading in the summer vacation, any of Hegel, the *Wellesley Magazine*, and Bishop Stubbs' Constitutional History of England.

NORUMBEGA SENIOR.—The technical name of "the little black spot" in the eye of a fish, is the iris. If you desire any information as to its use, "ask yourself."

INQUIRING FACULTY.—We cannot say that we are in favor of voluntary chapel. The pernicious effect of this system is clearly shown on pages 177 and 178.

INEXPERIENCE.—We consider the following recipes thoroughly reliable.

Argument à la Boulanger: Take one question which cannot possibly be decided, either affirmatively or negatively. Add one or two definitions from the Century Dictionary. Gather not less than fifty good, bad, and indifferent articles on both sides of the subject. Mix thoroughly. Let simmer for a week or two, and set aside to clarify. Then mass your material well, and flavor with concrete evidence. Serve clear, with persuasion, and garnish plentifully with authorities.

Petition to the Academic Council: Roll a wish, real or fancied, in a mixture of respect and humility. Spread evenly over a large sheet of paper. Garnish with red tape. This dish is rather difficult for beginners. Do not be discouraged by failure at first.

Daily Theme: Take any commonplace object; cover with a thick layer of description; smother in associations, and flavor with moral sentiments, cynical reflections, or soaring aspirations, according to taste. Sprinkle plentifully with references to the Ideal, and garnish with quotations. This will insure a "fairly successful" result.

Acceptance of Invitation to a Society: Cover gratified expectation—or, if that cannot be secured, disappointed hope—with a light froth of joyous surprise. Set aside to cool, until any appearance of hot haste is removed. A grain of flattery will make the dish more palatable to some.

Refus à la Mode,—a Cold Slaw-ter of Hopes: Take the green and tender hopes of a whole society. Crush them thoroughly; mould in conventional form. Serve with a dressing of lingering regret.

ECONOMICAL JUNIOR.—It certainly does pay to buy your cap and gown at the beginning of your Senior year. It will save you money, for

(1) It will be unnecessary to buy either a spring or fall wrap.
(2) The gown takes the place of a mackintosh on rainy days.
(3) It serves as an opera cloak on Monday evenings.
(4) It is the most dignified and convenient garment in which to appear when the fire alarm sounds at 2.30 A. M.,—even if worn upside down.
(5) It is a handy penwiper.
(6) It will increase the dignity you have, or take the place of that you have not.

Hark! hark!
The dogs do bark,
The Seniors are coming to town;
Some to work,
And some to shirk,
But all in cap and gown.

"Student, student, quite imprudent,
How does your record grow?"
"With Math. exams., and German crams,
And Forensics all in a row."

This Senior girl wrote petitions;
This Junior girl discussed.
This Soph'more girl made good resolutions;
This Freshman girl said, "I must."
This Five-year girl said,
"Quee, quee, quee, I'm out of the fuss."

There was a young college with curriculum new;
She had so many students she didn't know what to do.
Some she sent to the village; to some she gave rooms;
And some she conditioned, and sent to their homes.

Little Bopeep
Has lost some sleep,
And doesn't know when she lost it.
Leave her alone,
And she'll go home
With all her nerves exhausted.

Young Mr. Love-to-Flirt
Tried with Miss Dove to flirt;
Manner not new.
The harder he tried, the softer he grew.

Wellesley, Wellesley, have you any boat?
"Yes, madam, that I have; best kind afloat."
One's for the Seniors, the Juniors have one,
And one's for the Sophomores, equaled by none."*

*Probably refers to "Sophomores," not to "boat." It is supposed that the exigencies of verse prevented the author from adding, "In their own estimation."

There was a young woman, as I have heard tell,
Who went to Wellesley her learning for to swell.
She went to Wellesley on registration day,
And she fell into Curriculum Way.

There came a philosopher whose name was Kant,
And showed her knowledge to be but scant.
He proved her knowledge to be so very small,
That what she thought she knew she knew, she didn't know at all.

When all this at last the young woman found out,
She became bewildered, she began to doubt;
She began to wonder, she began to cry,
"Lack o' mercy on me! Am I really I?

"If I be I, as I do hope I be,
There are things-in-themselves that I do see;
If I be I, they'll turn out to be real,
And if I be not I, they'll prove themselves ideal."

So when the young woman began to analyze,
Phenomena only met her searching eyes.
She became discouraged, she began to cry,
"Lack o' mercy on me! This is none of I!"

There was a young woman put on a committee;
Seventeen quires she wrote with two stubs.
"Why should you work so?" I asked her in pity,
For she held office in twenty-three clubs.

"Young woman, young woman, young woman," quoth I,
"O wherefore, O wherefore, O wherefore so spry?"
"I want to reform things from ocean to sky."
"But you'll break down, you know, by and by."

Little Jill Horner
Sat in a corner
Computing the value of -.
She sat up till twelve
In her problems to delve.
And said, "What a good girl am I!"

Little Miss Muffet
Sat on a tuffet
Cribbing her drawings for Zoo.
There came the Professor
And tried to address her,
And frightened Miss Muffet quite blue.

There was a young woman, and what do you think?
She scribbled with nothing but pencils and ink.
Pencils and ink were the chief thing she carried,
And yet this poor woman still hoped to be married.

Sing a song of Chapel.
Just at half past eight;
Four and twenty breathless girls
By a closed door—late.

When the door is opened,
Girls begin to sing.
Is not this a merry tale
Before the world to fling?

Little Miss Crooks
Has lost her books,
And she can't tell where to find them.
If she only roams
Through the Catacombs,
She will see where kind friends have assigned them.

The Magazine Board sat up in its tree.
Looking as happy as happy could be.
Till LEGENDA came by, and remarked with a grin,
We're not going to put your photograph in.
Hard times such as these mean economy's vise,
And we long ago planned that ourselves appear twice;
And if *we* appear twice, there'll be no room for *you*;
Don't cry, dears, for, prithee, what good will it do?

This is the College Beautiful.
This is the bell that rings in the morn,
And oft asunder dreams hath torn
For maidens fair and all forlorn,
By whom are brooms and dustpans borne,
Which sweep the matting, somewhat worn,
On the floors of the College Beautiful.

Baa, baa, Wellesley, have you got a rule?
Yes, sir, yes, sir, two whole pages full.
Part for the Seniors, Juniors too, and Sophs;
A lot for the Freshmen, but none at all for Profs.

When our good Steward ruled this land,   A bread pudding that steward made,
   He was a goodly king;   And put ten raisins in,
He gathered crusts, stale biscuits, too,   And for it cooked a wondrous sauce,
   To make a bread pudding.   All pink and white, and thin.

      No Faculty did eat thereof,
        Nor did a student munch;
      Yet what they could not eat that night,
        They had next day for lunch.

The President of '94 and sixty girls, one night,
Stayed in the P. L. R. three hours for naught, then winged their flight.

         TO Z A
   Little girl blue
    Come blow your horn,
   The Freshmen are coming   Three wise maids of Wellesley
    youth: ratpin.   Were alarmed by a mouse.
                                           If the mouse had been madder,
                                           My tale had been sadder.

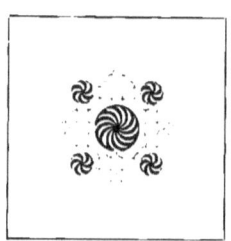

College Songs and Verse.

The Ideal.

THE CENTURY, APRIL, 1890.

BY the promise of noon's blue splendor in the dawn's first silvery gleam,
   By the song of the sea that compelleth the path of the rock-cleaving stream,
I summon thee, recreant dreamer, to rise and follow thy dream.

At the inmost core of thy being I am a burning fire,
From thine own altar-flame kindled, the hour when souls aspire;
For know that men's prayer shall be answered, and guard thy spirit's desire.

That which thou wouldst be thou must be; that which thou shalt be thou art.
As the oak, astir in the acorn, the dull earth rendeth apart,
Lo, thou, the seed of thy longing, that breaketh and waketh the heart.

Mine is the cry of the night wind, startling thy traitorous sleep;
Moaning, I echo thy music, and e'en while thou boastest to reap
Alien harvests, my anger resounds from the vehement deep.

I am the solitude folding thy soul in a sudden embrace;
Faint waxes the voice of thy fellow, wan the light on his face;
Life is as cloud-drift about thee alone in shelterless space.

I am the drawn sword barring the lanes thy mutinous feet
Vainly covet for greenness, loitering pace or fleet.
Thine is the crag path chosen; on the crest shall rest be sweet.

I am thy strong consoler, when the desolate human pain
Darkens upon thee, the azure out-blotted by rush of the rain.
All thou dost cherish may perish; still shall thy guest remain.

Call me thy foe in thy passion; claim me in peace for thy friend:
Yet bethink thee, by lowland or upland, wherever thou willest to wend,
I am thy angel of judgment; mine eyes thou must meet in the end.

—KATHARINE LEE BATES, '80.

A Song for To-day.

GROWETH the morning from gray to gold;
    Up, my heart, and greet the sun!
Yesterday's cares are a tale that is told,
    Yesterday's tasks are a work that is done.

Yesterday's failures are all forgot,
    Buried beneath the billows of sleep.
Yesterday's burdens are as they were not;
    Lay them low in the soundless deep.

Share thy crust, and ask no dole;
    Offer the cup thou wouldst never drain.
Only he who saveth his soul
    Loseth all that he fain would gain.

Smile with him who has gained his desire;
    Smile the gladder if at thy cost.
It was his to win and thine to aspire;
    It is his to-day who loved the most.

Pluck the flower that blooms at thy door;
    Cherish the love that the day may send;
Cometh an hour when all thy store
    Vainly were offered for flower or friend.

Gratefully take what life offereth,
    Looking to heaven nor seeking reward.
So shalt thou find, come life, come death,
    Earth and the sky are in sweet accord.

—LOUISE MANNING HODGKINS

Four-o'clocks.

IT was that they loved the children,
   The children used to say;
   For there was no doubt
   That when school was out,
At the same time every day,
   Down by the wall,
   Where the grass grew tall,
Under the hedge of the hollyhocks,
   One by one,
   At the touch of the sun,
There opened the four-o'clocks.

It was that they loved the children,—
   But the children have gone away;
   And somebody goes
   When nobody knows,
At the same time every day,
   To see by the wall,
   Where the grass grows tall,
Under the hedge of the hollyhocks,
   How, one by one,
   At the touch of the sun,
Still open the four-o'clocks.

—L. B., '94.

To My Mother.

STRONG daughter of the Truth, with uplift eyes
   To catch the sweetness of thy Father's face,
   And learn His will for thee, keep thou thy place
Far vanward, where the hymns of glory rise:
Guide, thou, my weaker footsteps, who art wise!
   Teach me to know the great and wondrous grace
   Of thy fine self-lessness, and speak apace
The word of life that in thy heart's depth lies.

Like Him who is the pattern for us all,
   Thou art, in less degree, the way, the life,
   The truth, to me, thy child. . . . No shades can creep
Along thy pathway, neither sound of strife
Fall on thine ear; for thy soul's peace, so deep,
   Is hid with Christ in God, beyond recall.

—M. G. M., '92.

Waking Song.
(AFTER THE PROVENÇAL.)

WELLESLEY PRELUDE.

FRESH the dawn is breaking,
   Purple grows the sky;
Orchard birds are waking,
Meadow grasses shaking
   Dewy banners dry.
Which, pray, think you is the sweetest,
Day that lingers, or night that is fleetest?

All the silver night,
   All the night of May,
Apple blossoms bright
Drifted clear and white,
   In the moonbeams lay.
Which, pray, think you is the sweetest,
Day that lingers or night that is fleetest?

Wan the wind flowers wait,
   Petal opal-tinted;
At the Orient gate
Comes their king in state;
   Gold his auguries glinted.
Which, pray, think you is the sweetest,
Day that lingers, or night that is fleetest?

—FLORENCE WILKINSON, '92.

At Twilight.

BOSTON TRANSCRIPT.

ALL day I walk in labor's dusty ways,
    And find in present work my joy; at eve,
Of care and toil, not loath, I take my leave,
And on my quiet couch give place to praise!
Far upward to the shadowy blue I gaze,
    And watch the stars the great sun's loss retrieve.
My soul, in one, doth past and future weave,
And Hope and Mercy chant accordant lays.
The souls I love, distant however far,
    Come forth like stars that brilliant day hath hid,
And look with large, kind, comprehending eyes,
Upon me through the gloom, serene and wise.
    How can I lonely be, those friends amid
Whose love no change of time or place can mar?

—JOSEPHINE A. CASS, '80.

Out on the Cliffs at Twilight.

OUT on the cliffs at twilight,
  With sea-winds in one's hair,
    The breadth and sweep
    Of the mighty deep,
And the sigh of the ocean's prayer.
    One hears it confess
    Its sinfulness
In the sob of its ebb and flow,
    While soft—sweet,—
    Close at one's feet,
The waters come and go.

Out on the cliffs at twilight,
  The flowers their silence keep;
    The roses fold
    Their hearts of gold
In their petals, and go to sleep;
    But their fragrant prayer
    Is in all the air,
As they rustle to and fro,
    While soft—sweet,—
    Close at one's feet,
The waters come and go.

Out on the cliffs at twilight,
  Only one's self and God,
    A lone star-ray
    Athwart the way
That no man's foot has trod.
    Will He hear up there,
    If one says a prayer?
The fireflies flit and glow,
    While soft—sweet,—
    Close at one's feet,
The waters come and go.

—L. B., '94.

Attic Glimpses.

OVER the city the mist looms gray;
    Smoke from the chimneys is shifting and streaming;
    The gilded Cross on the spire is gleaming—
A single rift in the cloudswept day;
And over the city the mist looms gray.

The red brick rows stand gaunt and grim—
    Sentinel posts of trade's contriving;
    While faces seamed with its craft and striving
Peer from the dark to the daylight dim,
Where the red brick rows stand gaunt and grim.

An April swallow is floating slow
    High o'er the roofs and the yellow river;
    Careless is he of the hearts that quiver
Where hurrying feet past the bridges go—
The April swallow is floating slow.

Onward presses the pilgrim throng;
    None shall know of the goal that awaits them,—
    None but the Dreamer whose dream creates them.
Pouring His thought through the world along
As onward presses the pilgrim throng.

Above them Justice the balance holds,
    Her tall white form from the prison lifting;
    Little she recks of the shadows drifting—
She whom the bandage of blindness folds;
Above them Justice her balance holds.

All we would know the fog shuts out:
    What of the heart of the day's dull history—
    Glory or gloom at the core of the mystery?
Madness or vision the truth of the doubt?
But all we would know the fog shuts out.

Over the city the mist looms gray;
    Smoke from the chimneys is shifting and streaming;
    The gilded Cross on the spire is gleaming—
A single rift in the cloudswept day;
And over the city the mist looms gray.

—Lillian Corbett Barnes, '91.

THE night is drear and the stars are dim,
    There's a feeble moon o'erhead;
And a gray mist clings to the rigid earth
    Like a face cloth over the dead.

I must find my way through the trackless vague,
    Though I'm loath, I'm loath to go;
I must leave the light and the life I love,
    For I died an hour ago.

An hour ago, at my lightest word
    They had given their lives for me;
Now I call in vain, for their ears are deaf,
    And my tears they cannot see.

I know I am dead, for my form lies there,
    And my friends are weeping around,
And I clasp them in vain with shadowy hands,
    And my voice has lost its sound.

There is no place left in the world I knew,
    'Midst the friends I loved, for me;
They are blind and deaf, and the earth is cold,
    And the night is gloomy to see.

I must wander forth through the cheerless mist,
    Though the way I cannot know;
And there's never a friend or a ray of light:
    Oh, I'm loath, I'm loath to go!

Vespers.

THE obedient throb of the music
    Responds to the ivory keys
Like a prisoner unresisting
    Through despair of its release:
And aloft, with a holy radiance
    Divine with the Sabbath peace,
The gold of the college motto
    Is gleaming down,
And the lights above the altar
    Are a crown.

One shuts one's eyes, and the music
    Still throbs to the ivory keys,
'Till it throbs itself into memories
    Whose voices never cease;
And one's heart goes silently with it
    Into other scenes than these.
The gold of the college motto
    Is gleaming down,
And the lights above the altar
    Are a crown.

On Reading Poe's "Ligeia."

The Literary World, 1880.

BEHOLD a lonely turret chamber, hung
    With gleaming tapestries, whereon are wrought
    Dark arabesques, that mock the gazer's thought,
By subtle change to demon shapes. High swung
A lamp of twisted gold, with many a tongue
    Of serpent flame: swift apparitions, caught
    And prisoned fast in carven ebony: naught
Save leaden windows, whence no light is wrung.
What means this horror of enchanted gloom?
    O wizard poet, what this sound of woe?
This weird, low music of the wailing wind,
Sweeps ever round the ever-darkening room!
    "Behold, the open mystery doth show
The haunted chamber of the poet's mind!"

—Marion Pelton Guild, '80.

At Sea.

BOSTON TRANSCRIPT, NOVEMBER, 1888.

OH, splendid is the wide, unbroken reach of sky!
    Splendid the one great sapphire of the sea!
The lone white gull is flitting homeless by,
    And the wild waves exult in Titan glee!
And with a strong, incessant, tireless motion,
    Like a soul-purpose which no doubt assails,
The mighty ship advances o'er the ocean.

But I am weary for a quiet nook of land,
    Full of tall maples and light-swaying ferns;
The mountains guard it tenderly, a giant band,
    And safe within the red field-lily burns,
Like flames on Summer's altar. I am longing
    For silent steadfastness of solemn hills,
Where vain ambitions will no more come thronging.

—JOSEPHINE A. CASS, '80.

A Friendship.

SMALL fellowship of daily commonplace
    We hold together, dear, constrained to go
    Diverging ways. Yet day by day I know
    My life is sweeter for thy life's sweet grace;
And if we meet but for a moment's space,
    Thy touch, thy word, sets all the world aglow.
    Faith soars serener, haunting doubts shrink low,
    Abashed before the sunshine of thy face.
Nor press of crowd, nor waste of distance, serves
    To part us. Every hush of evening brings
Some hint of thee, true-hearted friend of mine;
And as the farther planet thrills and swerves
    When toward it through the darkness Saturn swings,
Even so my spirit feels the spell of thine.

            —ELLEN BURROUGHS.

College Songs.

Ninety-Four Crew Song.

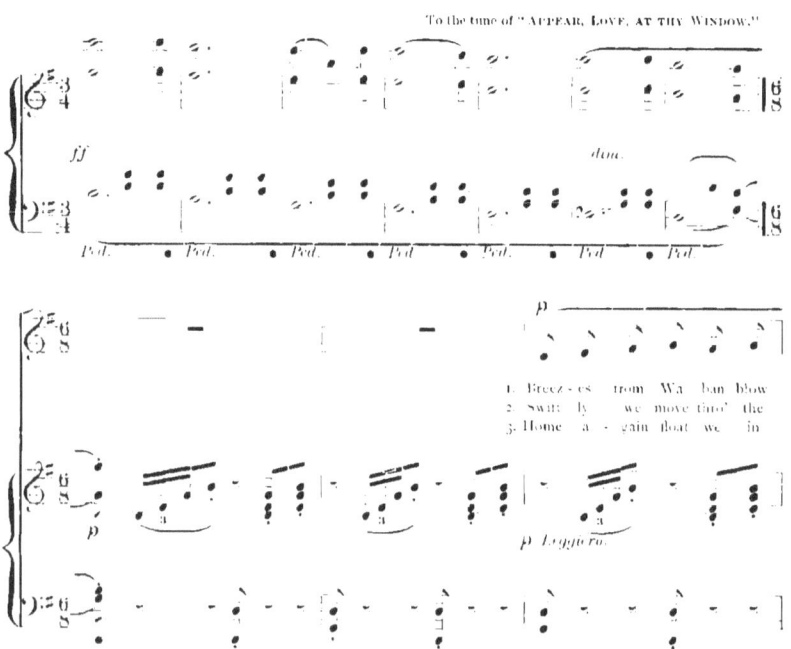

Ninety-Four Crew Song.

Ninety-Four Crew Song.

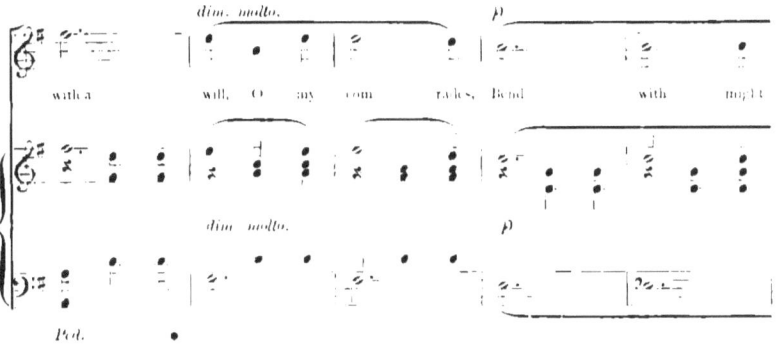
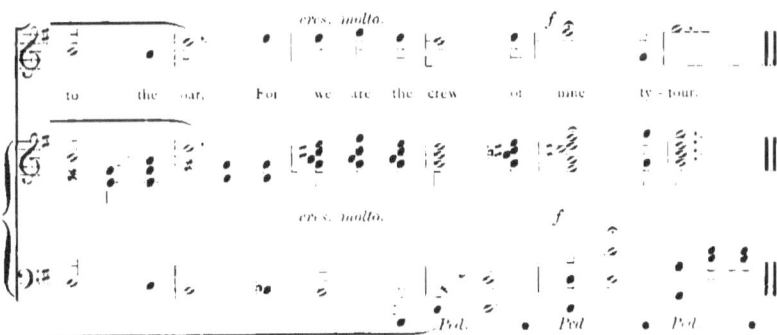

Boo! Hoo!

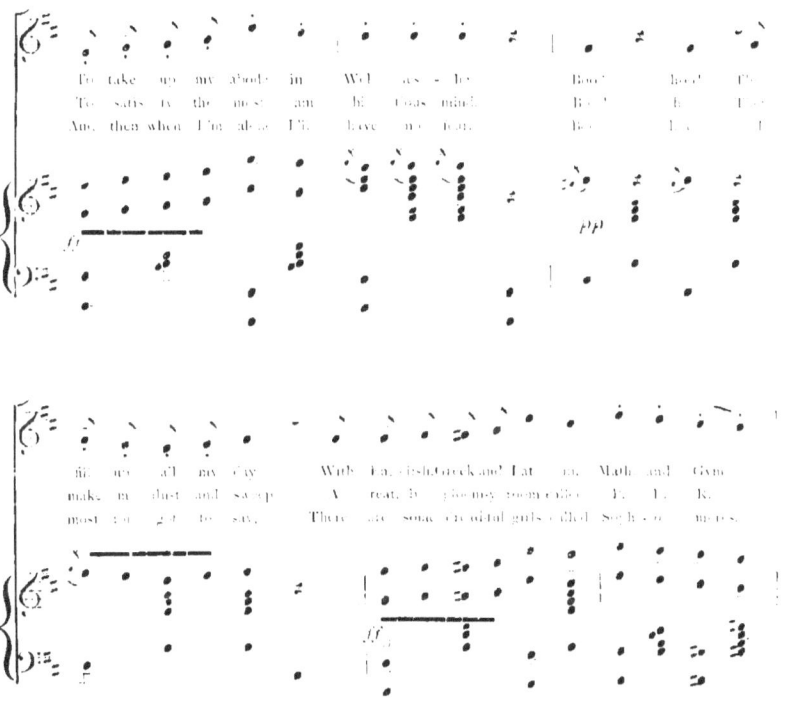

Boo! Hoo!

Wellesley Mother Goose.

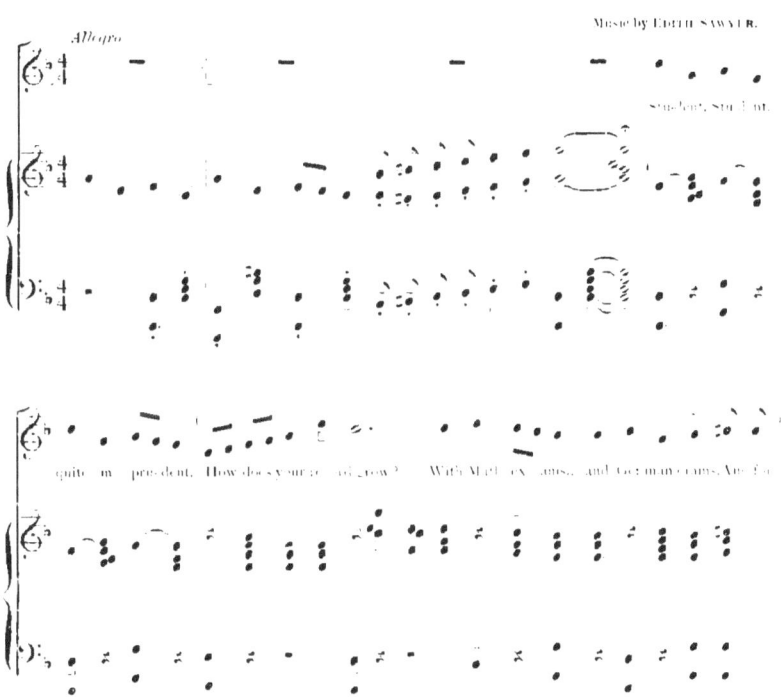

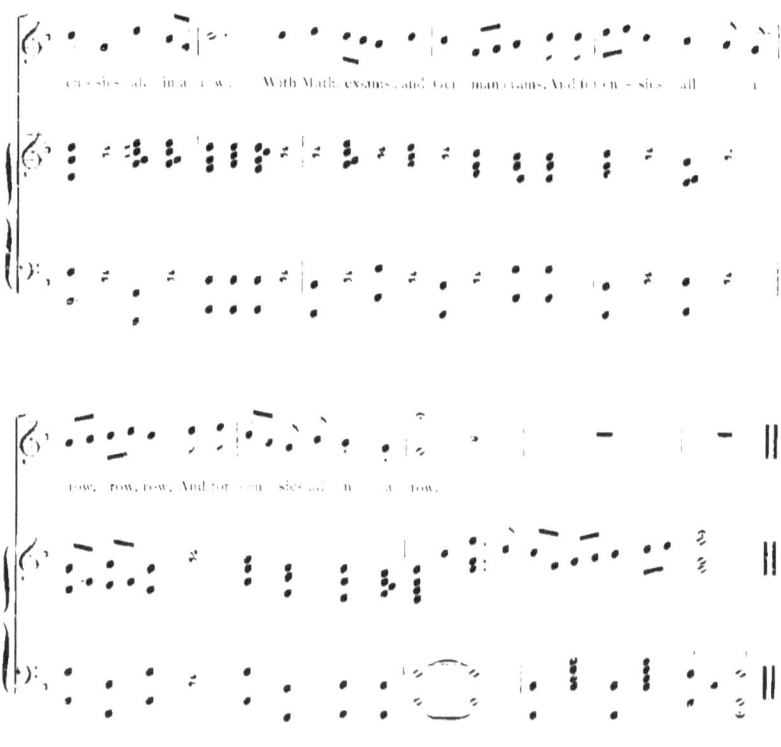
Wellesley, Mother Goose.

Little Jill Horner.

Music by ELIGH SAWYER

Little Jill Horner.

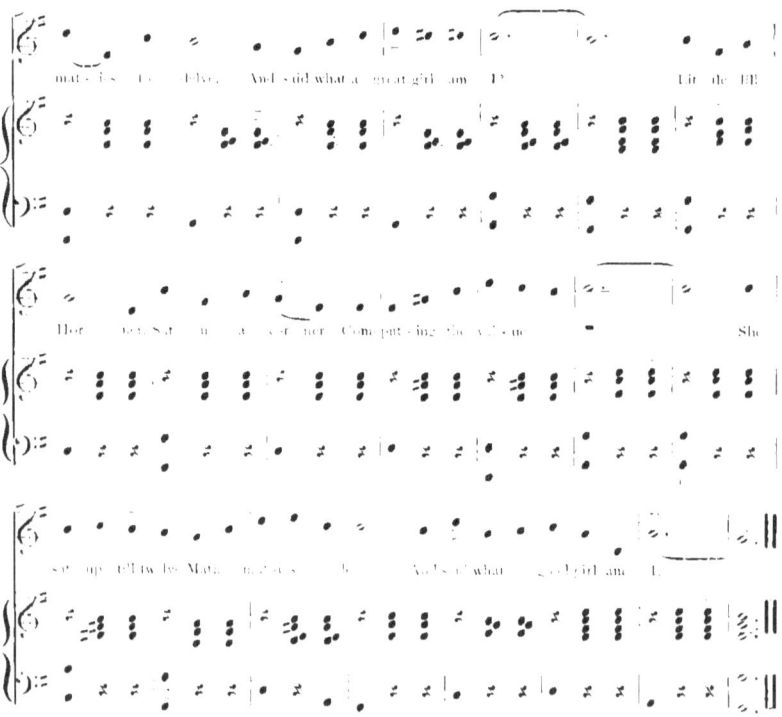

My College Girl.

Words by ALICE WELCH KELLOGG.

Music by JUSTUS W. HITZ
for the WELLESLEY GLEE CLUB.

1. She is skilled in Math-e-mat-ics, And knows more of Hy-dro-sta-tics Than I learned in all my plod-ding years at Yale; She per-forms ex-per-i-ments, With the di-vers el-e-ments, That would
2. She can French and Ger-man speak, And can write in an-cient Greek, Get-ting all the va-rious ac-cents quite cor-rect, Though she deals hard blows at Russians, In his-tor-i-cal discussions, Not a
3. She, al-though 'tis not her hab-it, Can dis-sect a good-sized rab-bit, Giv-ing you the name of each and ev-'ry bone; And she knows a plant or tree, On the land or in the sea, Slight-ing

My College Girl.

(musical score)

... make her lit-tle broth-er's cheeks turn pale. She per-
... flaw in all her log-ic I de-tect. Though she
... not meanwhile the all im-por-tant stone. And she

... forms ex-per-i-ments, With the di-vers el-e-ments, That would
... deals hard blows at Russians, In his-tor-i-cal dis-cussions, Not a
... knows a plant or tree, On the land or in the sea, Slight-ing

... make her lit-tle broth-er's cheeks turn pale.
... flaw in all her log-ic I de-tect.
... not meanwhile the all im-por-tant stone.

4. Like a statue she can pose,
And interpret learned prose
In a way that makes my pulses wildly beat.
:She has studied poetry lyric,
Epic also, and satiric,
Till her diction and her style are quite complete:

5. More than all, the little sinner,
She can cook as good a dinner
As a hungry man would ever wish to spy.
:And I challenge the world over,
If two folks they can discover,
Quite so happy as my college girl and I:

Table of Contents.

FRONTISPIECE
TITLE PAGE
DEDICATION
EDITORIAL BOARD:
    Photographs
    Autographs
PREFACE
FOUNDERS OF WELLESLEY, THE
GLIMPSES OF MISS SHAFER
OFFICERS OF GOVERNMENT AND INSTRUCTION
ALUMNAE AND CLASSES
SOCIETIES
    Shakespeare
    Phi Sigma
    Zeta Alpha
    Tau Zeta Epsilon
    Agora
    Classical
ORGANIZATIONS
PUBLICATIONS
TREE DAY
MUSICAL SOCIETIES
SPORTS AND PASTIMES
EDITORIALS
COLLEGE CALENDAR
COLLEGE VIEWS
NOTES AND QUERIES
ANSWERS TO CORRESPONDENTS
CHILDREN'S DEPARTMENT
COLLEGE VERSE
COLLEGE SONGS
ADVERTISEMENTS

Hark! Hark! The gong doth sound,
The **Ads** are coming along.
Some sell hats and some sell gowns,
But all sell for a song!

Index to Advertisements.

	PAGE		PAGE
Albany Teachers' Agency	54	Drewsen's Dyeing Establishment	50
American and Foreign Teachers' Bureau	21	Duckett, Dominick	31
Babbitt, B. T.	46	Eastern Teachers' Agency	41
Bailey's Hotel	27	Eimer & Amend	6
Barclay Company	50	Fall River Line	18
Bardeen, C. W.	45	Fisk Teachers' Agency	3
Bates-O'Brien Manufacturing Co	49	French, Abram, Company	5
Bausch and Lomb Optical Company	35	Grace, James J.	49
Boston and Albany R.R.	22	Grimmer, C. P.	3
Bridge Teachers' Agency	41	Hall, Martin L. & Co.	24
Briggs, Richard & Co	41	Harcourt Place Seminary, Gambier, Ohio,	36
Broad, H.	25	Haskell, H. C	33
Brooks Bros.	43	Hearn, Charles W	37
Burlen, Robert	34	Hinds, A. S.	14
Burnett, Joseph & Co.	39	Hollander, L. P. & Co.	5
Burr, H. M.	33	Hollings, R. & Co.	25
Butler, Wm. S. & Co	20	Holmes, The, Company	10
Cambridge School, Cambridge, Mass.	45	Horsman, E. I.	55
Capen, Sprague & Co	30	Houghton & Dutton	7
Carter, H. H.	45	Houghton, Mifflin & Co.	32
Chandler & Co.	44	Howard Seminary, West Bridgewater, Mass.	17
Chessman, Geo. H. & Co.	26	International News Company	47
Clapp, Otis & Son	30	Jenkins, O. A. & Co.	3
Clark, A. B.	43	Jenkins, Wm. R.	49
Conant, M. J. & Co.	11	John P Lovell Arms Company	40
Cotrell & Leonard	26	Jones, McDuffee & Stratton	18
Cowdrey, F. T., Company	51	Kakas & Sons	28
Cutler Bros. & Co.	24	Kennedy's Champion Biscuits	12
Dana Hall School	20	Lake Shore, Michigan Southern Railway,	56
De Wolfe, Fiske & Co.	42	Lamson & Hubbard	10
Dreka	21	Lawrence, H. L. & Co.	35

Continued on page 4.

O. A. JENKINS & CO.

SUCCESSORS TO GEO. N. BIGELOW & COMPANY

407 Washington Street, Boston.

FINE HATS, RICH FURS.

Sole Boston Agents for Connelly's New York Round
Hats and Pattern Bonnets.

Special Designs in High-grade Millinery.   Walking and Sailor Hats a Specialty.

FURRIERS AND LADIES HATTERS   O. A. JENKINS & CO.

C. P. GRIMMER,   The Fisk Teachers' Agencies.

Everett O. Fisk & Co., Proprietors.

🌸 FLORIST 🌸

PRESIDENT.
Everett O. Fisk,   4 Ashburton Place, Boston, Mass.

MANAGERS.
W. B. Herrick,   4 Ashburton Place, Boston, Mass.
A. G. Fisher,   4 Ashburton Place, Boston, Mass.
I. H. Andrews,   4 Ashburton Place, Boston, Mass.
Martha Hoyt,   4 Ashburton Place, Boston, Mass.
Helen G. Eager,   4 Ashburton Place, Boston, Mass.
H. E. Crocker,   70 Fifth Avenue, New York, N. Y.
W. O. Pratt,   7 Fifth Avenue, New York, N. Y.
B. F. Clark,   150 Wabash Avenue, Chicago, Ill.
I. C. Hicks,   Room 3, 131 Third Street, Portland, Or.
C. C. Boynton,   525 & 526 Spring St., Los Angeles, Cal.
W. O. McTaggart, 32 Church Street, Toronto, Can.

Send to any of the above agencies for 100-page Agency
Manual. Correspondence with employers invited. Registration forms sent to teachers on application.

37 WEST STREET,

Boston, Mass.

Choice Cut Flowers.

TELEPHONE 1559.

Index to Advertisements

CONTINUED.

	PAGE		PAGE
LEVILLY & FLECKENSTEIN	48	SELIGMAN, J. & Co.	31
LLOYD, ANDREW J.	26	SHATTUCK & JONES	51
McGILLIVRAE, L. K.	42	SHEPARD, NORWELL & Co.	7
MERRIAM, G. & C. COMPANY	54	SHREVE, CRUMP & LOW	7
MERRILL PIANO Co.	39	SILVER, BURDETT & Co.	49
MICHIGAN CENTRAL R. R.	57	SOULE PHOTOGRAPH COMPANY	11
MOSELEY, T. E. & Co.	24	SPRINGER BROS.	53
NORTH PACKING AND PROVISION Co.	47	SQUIRE, JOHN P. & Co.	16
NOURSE'S SCHOOL, MISS, Cincinnati, Ohio	36	STATISTICS	9, 15, 19, 23, 27, 29, 33
NOYES BROS.	32	ST. DENIS HOTEL, N. Y.	48
OLIVER BROS.	25	STEARNS, R. H.	19
PACKER'S TAR SOAP	27	STOWELL, A. & Co.	17
PERRY, CHAS. W.	30	STURTEVANT & HALEY	13
PHENYO-CAFFEIN Co.	54	TAILBY, J. & SON	37
PISO CONSUMPTION CURE	48	THORP & MARTIN Co.	12
PLUMMER, GEO. A. & Co.	36	THURSTON, JOHN H.	6
PLYMPTON, LUCY A.	58	TUTTLE, H. H. & Co.	11
POND'S EXTRACT COMPANY	28	VERSE	38, 52
RAYMOND & WHITCOMB	42	WADSWORTH, HOWLAND & Co.	6
READ, WM. & SON	58	WALNUT HILL SCHOOL, Natick, Mass.	43
RICHARDSON & DE LONG BROS.	8	WARD, SAMUEL, Co.	21
ROCHESTER LAMP Co.	55	WASHBURN, O. J.	20
ROYAL BAKING POWDER	39	WEBER PIANO Co.	58
RUMFORD CHEMICAL WORKS	17	WILLARD HALL SCHOOL, Danvers, Mass.	45
SAWYER, G. A.	16	WOOD, FRANK	34

The Wellesley Legenda.

L. P. HOLLANDER & CO.,
NOS. 202 TO 212 BOYLSTON STREET, AND PARK SQUARE, BOSTON.
ALSO 290 FIFTH AVENUE, NEW YORK.

ORDER DEPARTMENTS:
Costumes, Coats, Riding Habits, Millinery.

READY-MADE DEPARTMENTS:
Capes, Coats, Traveling Wraps; Dresses for Street,
Outing and House Wear; Trimmed Hats.

FINE DRESS GOODS, GLOVES, PARASOLS, UNDERWEAR.

SAMPLES AND PRICES SENT ON APPLICATION.

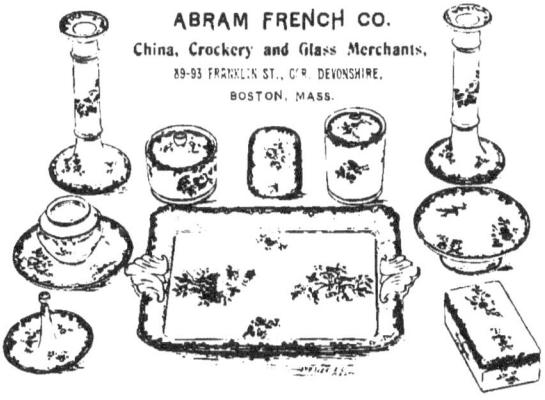

ABRAM FRENCH CO.
China, Crockery and Glass Merchants,
89-93 FRANKLIN ST., COR. DEVONSHIRE,
BOSTON, MASS.

**BUREAU AND BOUDOIR
...SETS...**

CONSISTING OF
Comb and Brush Tray, Pen
Tray, Pin Tray, Puff Box,
Powder Box, Paste Box,
Match Box, Stamp Box, Ink
Stand, Ring Stand, Tall Can-
dlesticks, Low Candlesticks.

TO BE SOLD IN SETS OR SINGLE PIECES.

These Bureau Sets come in Havi-
land and Carlsbad ware, also in old patterns very desirable and useful.

Wedding, Engagement,
Anniversary, and Compliment-
ary Gifts a Specialty.
Also Prize Cups.

The Wellesley Legenda.

ESTABLISHED 1851

EIMER & AMEND

Manufacturers
and Importers of

**CHEMICALS and
CHEMICAL APPARATUS**

205, 207, 209, and 211 Third Avenue
Corner of 18th Street
NEW YORK

Photographic Outfits

And
Supplies of all kinds.

❀

Developing, Printing and Bromide Enlargements.
Collections of Photographs mounted in Albums.
Stereopticons, Lanterns and Slides for sale or rental.

❀

JOHN H. THURSTON,

50 Bromfield St. (second floor),
BOSTON.

Artists' :::
Materials

INCLUDING
COLORS FOR OIL, WATER-COLOR, CHINA, AND TAPESTRY PAINTING
MATERIALS FOR CRAYON AND CHARCOAL DRAWING
CANVAS, BRUSHES, EASELS, MODELING TOOLS, ETC.
ART STUDIES AND BOOKS OF INSTRUCTION

DRAFTING INSTRUMENTS Either Singly or in Sets

DRAWING AND BLUE PROCESS PAPERS, SCALES, TRIANGLES, CURVES, AND T-SQUARES

Wadsworth, Howland & Co. (Incorporated)
82, 84 WASHINGTON STREET, BOSTON, MASS.

The Wellesley Legenda.

HOUGHTON & DUTTON.

PHOTOGRAPH MATERIALS.—Our prices on everything in this line are the lowest in Boston, and we carry a full assortment of all desirable articles. As a specimen of some of our low prices, we quote the following:

Celluloid Developing Trays.				Hard Rubber Trays.			
4 x 5	5 x 8	6½ x 8½	8 x 10	4 x 5	5 x 8	6½ x 8½	8 x 10
43c.	63c.	78c.	$1.05	24c.	40c.	63c.	98c.

Omega Paper.				Bromide Paper.			

The best of all Ready Sensitized Papers. We receive it fresh from the maker semi-weekly, and are authorized by them to guarantee every sheet. If it will not work well we replace it with new.

4 x 5	5 x 8	6½ x 8½	4 x 5 per gross.
18c.	35c.	80c.	$1.50

All Other Sizes in Proportion.

4 x 5	5 x 7	5 x 8	6½ x 8½
21c.	35c.	39c.	58c.

All Other Sizes in Proportion.

Cameras, Lenses, Shutters, Plates, Chemicals, etc., etc., of every description, at the lowest prices in the world.

Corner Tremont and Beacon Streets, BOSTON.

SHREVE, CRUMP & LOW COMPANY

147 Tremont Street, Boston.

Diamonds, Watches, Gems.

Canes, Umbrellas.

FINEST STOCK OF STATIONERY
CLASS-DAY INVITATIONS
COLLEGE PRINTING OF EVERY DESCRIPTION

Shepard, Norwell & Co.

When you wish to buy

Gloves, Laces, Hoisery, Art Drapery Silks, Fretwork, Screens

Or any kind of

∴ DRY GOODS ∴

Visit

Shepard, Norwell & Co.'s

Winter Street, Boston.

Goods sent by addressing our Mail Order Department
YOU ARE SURE OF HONEST DEALING.

The Wellesley Legenda.

LINKY-DINKY-DIDO.

A COLLEGE SONG.

"Hi, hi" conductor, hi!" she cried;
He stopped the car, she stepped inside,
Sang linky, dinky, dido.
Whereon a man jumped to his feet,
Remarking, "Madam, here's a seat;"
And she replied with manner sweet,
"O linky, dinky, dido."

"O linky—what?" inquired the man;
"Why, linky, dido," she began;
"O linky, dinky, dido."
"Ah!" he exclaimed, with pulse astir,
"Am I correct if I infer
Your way of saying 'Thank you, sir,'
Is, 'Linky, dinky, dido'?"

"Oh no," she laughed, with manner gay;
"That's not my purpose when I say,
'My linky, dinky, dido.'
I'm trying to evolve a song
To celebrate with praises strong
That Hook and Eye they call DeLong,
With linky, dinky, dido."

"Let me assist," the fellow said,
And straight she followed as he led
With linky, dinky, dido.
"Hear Gabriel shout his final trump;
Perfection can no higher jump,
And here's an instance, see that HUMP!
O linky, dinky, dido."

8

Summary of Students by States and Countries.

UNITED STATES.		UNITED STATES.	
Massachusetts	244	Indiana	
New York	78	Oregon	
Pennsylvania	45	Maryland	
Connecticut	36	Colorado	
New Hampshire	36	Tennessee	
New Jersey	36	Louisiana	
Illinois	35	South Dakota	
Ohio	35	Wisconsin	
Maine	29	Alabama	
Vermont	23	Georgia	
Rhode Island	19	Montana	
Missouri	17	South Carolina	
District of Columbia	14	Texas	
Iowa	12	Virginia	
Kentucky	10	NOVA SCOTIA	
Kansas	7	CEYLON	
Michigan	7	INDIA	
California	6	JAPAN	
Minnesota	6	Total	

The Wellesley Legenda.

Lamson and Hubbard — Manufacturing Furriers and Hatters
90 and 92 Bedford St.
Boston, Mass.

THE HOLMES CO.

Manufacturers

Ladies' Union Undergarments
AND
Fine Bathing Suits.

CLASS OF BOAT CREW

..SWEATERS..

40 TEMPLE PLACE,

Boston.

The Wellesley Legenda.

M. J. CONANT & CO.
COMMISSION DEALERS IN
BUTTER, CHEESE, EGGS, AND BEANS

21 and 22 South Market Street, 27 Chatham Street

M. J. CONANT.
W. S. VINCENT.

BOSTON, MASS.

STUDENTS CAN FIND AT OUR STORE
A CHOICE SELECTION OF FINE AND MEDIUM GRADE
Boots, Tennis and Gymnasium Shoes
Walking Shoes in all the new styles, including the "BLUCHER"

DISCOUNT TO
STUDENTS AND FACULTY.

HENRY H. TUTTLE & CO.
435 Washington Street, Boston, Mass.

UNMOUNTED PHOTOGRAPHS OF
Ancient and Modern Works of Art
Representing the Masterpieces of Painting, Sculpture and Architecture

VIEWS FROM ALL PARTS OF THE WORLD

Mounted Photographs for framing in great variety; all the new subjects as fast as published. Artists' materials for sale. Over 14,000 subjects in stock. Mail orders receive prompt attention. In writing, mention the LEGENDA.

Soule Photograph Company
338 WASHINGTON STREET
BOSTON

WE MAKE A SPECIALTY OF

Fine Steel Engraving and Embossing.

The latest and correct styles in Engraved Calling Cards, Invitations, Etc. Samples and estimates cheerfully furnished.

We Make a SPECIAL OFFER to furnish a Monogram, or Two-line Street Die, and Two Quires Finest Paper, and Envelopes Embossed, for $2.68.

THORP & MARTIN CO., Manufacturing Stationers,

No. 12 MILK STREET.   Successors to Winkley, Dresser & Company.

KENNEDY'S
CHAMPION
BISCUIT...

Have
You tried them?

The Wellesley Legenda.

STURTEVANT & HALEY
BEEF AND SUPPLY COMPANY

Wholesale and Retail Dealers in

Beef, Pork, Lard, and Hams,

Smoked and Dried Beef,
Smoked, Corned, and Saltpetered
Tongues. Tripe, Sausages, Etc.

38 AND 40 FANEUIL HALL MARKET,
BOSTON.

Slaughter House,
No. 11 Brighton Abattoir.

R. H. STURTEVANT, Treasurer and Manager.

The Wellesley Legenda.

A Fair Skin

Can always be ensured if, after exposure to the sun and rough winds, ladies will use

Hinds' Honey and Almond Cream.

It is particularly recommended for

Chapped Hands,

Face and Lips, Rough, Hard or Irritated Skin, Pimples, Scaly Eruptions, Wrinkles, Chilblains, Burns, Scalds, Wounds, Chafing, Ivy Poison, Stings and Bites of Insects, Inflamed and Irritated Piles, Salt Rheum, Eczema, and all the various conditions of the Skin of like character.

The Superiority of
Hinds' Honey and Almond Cream

Consists in its wonderful purifying and healing properties and cleanliness.

It is unlike any other preparation for the SKIN AND COMPLEXION, in that it contains no Oils, Greasy substances or Chemicals, neither Starchy or Mucilaginous principles to obstruct the pores of the skin; is quickly absorbed, leaving no trace of its use, and cannot injure the most delicate or sensitive skin.

A Sample Bottle FREE by mentioning this Book.

PREPARED ONLY BY

A. S. HINDS, Portland, Me.

Courses of Study, Offered.

Greek	9	Chemistry	
Latin	4	Physics	
German	16	Geology	
French	5	Mineralogy	
Italian	1	Botany	
Rhetoric and Composition	5	Zoology	
Philology	3	Pedagogics	
English Literature	9	Bibliography	
Philosophy	8	Elocution	
History	10	Bible	
Political Economy	4	Music	
History of Art	4	Art	
Mathematics	5		

THE BOSTON COOKING SCHOOL...

Established 1842
Incorporated 1892

Use and recommend

 **Squire's**
Pure Leaf Lard

It pays to use the Purest foods, as purity is essential to health. Nothing can equal the Pure Leaf, tried out in the old-fashioned way.

Our Name on the Package a Guarantee of Purity

JOHN P. SQUIRE & CO., Boston, Mass.

G. A. SAWYER...

Receiver and Dealer in

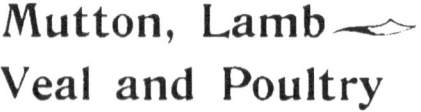

Mutton, Lamb
Veal and Poultry

BASEMENT NO. 3 FANEUIL HALL MARKET...

Slaughtering Establishment at
Watertown, Mass.

BOSTON, MASS.

Brain=Workers.

HORSFORD'S ACID PHOSPHATE

is recommended by physicians of all schools, for restoring brain force or nervous energy, in all cases where the nervous system has been reduced below the normal standard by overwork, as found in lawyers, teachers, students and brain-workers generally.

Dr. C. H. Goodman, St. Louis, says: "I have used it for several years, with especially good results in nervous prostration, the result of mental efforts; also in sleepless conditions of brain-workers."

Descriptive pamphlet free on application to

Beware of Substitutes and Imitations.   RUMFORD CHEMICAL WORKS, Providence, R. I.
For Sale by all Druggists.

The Wellesley Legenda.

Fine China, Glass and Lamps.

THE subscribers offer an extensive stock of the best products of English, French, German, Austrian, and Domestic Potteries and Glass Factories,—embracing every household requisite in this line.

IN the Art Pottery Rooms (third floor, take lift) will be seen choice specimens adapted to WEDDING GIFTS; also an extensive exhibit of ENGAGEMENT CUPS AND SAUCERS, from the low cost to the most expensive specimens.

JONES, McDUFFEE & STRATTON,

Fine China, Glass and Lamps.

Seven Floors
Inspection Invited

120 FRANKLIN STREET, BOSTON, MASS.

FALL RIVER LINE.
Boston and New York

STEAMERS:
Puritan, Pilgrim, Plymouth, and Providence.

PULLMAN VESTIBULED EXPRESS TRAIN composed of Parlor Cars and regular passenger coaches, leaves Park Square Station, Boston, week days, at 6 P. M., running through to steamer at Fall River in eighty minutes. Due in New York 7.30 A. M. Annex boat connection between Pier 28, North River, and Jersey City and Brooklyn, on arrival.

Splendid Orchestra on each Steamer.

Tickets, Staterooms, etc., secured at

No. 3 Old State House, corner Washington and State Streets, and at

Park Square Station, Boston.

J. R. KENDRICK,   GEO. L. CONNOR,
Gen. Manager.   Gen. Pass. Ag't.

L. H. PALMER, Agent, No. 3 Old State House,
BOSTON, MASS.

Shore Line (All Rail) Route to New York.

9 A. M.— Colonial Express) Week days, Boston to Washington without change. Buffet Smoker, Buffet Drawing-room and Day Coaches.

10 A. M — Bay State Limited) Week days, due in New York 3 P. M. A Vestibuled train composed entirely of parlor cars and parlor smoking car. Buffet service.

10.3 A. M.— Day Express Week days, due New York 4.30 P. M. Buffet Parlor Cars and through coaches.

1 P. M.— Afternoon Express Week days, due New York 7.3 P. M. Buffet Parlor Cars and through coaches.

3 P. M.— Shore Line Express Week days, due New York 9 P. M. Parlor Cars, Parlor Smoking car, and through coaches, with Dining car between Boston and New London.

5 P. M.— Gilt Edge Express Daily, due New York 11 P.M. Parlor cars, Parlor Smoking car, and through coaches, with Dining car between Boston and New London.

7 P. M.— Federal Express Daily, Boston to Washington without change. Pullman Vestibuled Sleeping cars and through coach to Philadelphia. Buffet service.

12 P. M.— Midnight Express Daily, due New York 7 A.M. Through Sleeping cars and "Allen" Compartment cars. Tickets, Drawing room car seats and Sleeping car berths secured at 3 Old State House, and at Park Square Station.

J. R. KENDRICK,   GEO. L. CONNOR,
Vice President.   *Pass. Traffic Manager.*
New York, New Haven & Hartford R.R.

L. H. PALMER, Agent, No. 3 Old State House, Boston, Mass.

The Average Age of Students by Classes.

	YEARS.	MONTHS.
Seniors	21	7
Juniors	20	6
Sophomores	19	10
Freshmen	18	10
Special Students	21	6

When You Reach Your Home, no matter what the distance from Boston, write to us whenever you are in need of any kind of Dry Goods. We shall always be glad to send samples, so far as the nature of the goods will allow. Your friends will want to know the best place to get Fine Goods.

R. H. STEARNS & COMPANY,
Boston, Mass.

The Wellesley Legenda.

William S. Butler & Company

Pattern Hats and Bonnets

...HIGH-CLASS MILLINERY NOVELTIES...

Nos. 90 to 98 Tremont Street
BOSTON, MASS.

Trimmed Millinery Department
Second Floor........

PARIS
No. 160 Rue Montmartre

Dana Hall School,
Wellesley, Mass.

❀❀

Thorough preparation for College work, with opportunities for advanced study in French, German and Music.

A new building will be ready for occupancy in September.

JULIA A. EASTMAN
SARAH P. EASTMAN
Principals

O. J. WASHBURN

Dentist

OFFICE....
ROOM 26 CLARK'S BLOCK

NATICK, MASS.

ESTABLISHED 1872

The Wellesley Legenda.

LOOK FOR THE WATERMARK — When purchasing your Society Writing Paper, and make sure it reads THE BOSTON LINEN

This is the leading Writing Paper for Society Correspondence

And is made in all the correct sizes, styles, and finishes, with Envelopes to match. Complete samples upon receipt of 4 cents in stamps if your dealer does not keep them.

SAMUEL WARD COMPANY
Paper Merchants, Stationers, Engravers, Printers
49 and 51 Franklin Street
BOSTON, MASS.
Proprietors of the celebrated Boston Linen,
Boston Bond and Bunker Hill Writing Papers.

AMERICAN
AND
FOREIGN TEACHERS'
BUREAU,

NO. 3 PARK STREET,
Boston, Mass.

...EIGHT YEARS ESTABLISHED...

We need teachers at all times for all departments of private school work.

DREKA
...Fine Stationery and Engraving House...
1121 Chestnut Street, Philadelphia.

COLLEGE INVITATIONS	WEDDING INVITATIONS
CLASS STATIONERY	VISITING CARDS
SOCIETY STATIONERY	BANQUET MENUS
PROGRAMMES, BADGES	DIPLOMAS AND MEDALS

STEEL PLATE ENGRAVING FOR FRATERNITIES, CLASSES AND COLLEGE ANNUALS

All work is executed in the establishment under the personal supervision of Mr. Dreka, and only in the best manner. Unequaled facilities and long, practical experience enable us to produce the newest styles and most artistic effects, while our reputation is a guarantee of the quality of the productions of this house.

Designs, Samples, and Prices sent on application.

The Wellesley Legenda.

FINEST ROAD BED ON THE CONTINENT

THROUGH CAR LINE
TO THE
West
Southwest
AND Northwest
Springfield Line...
.. BETWEEN ..

BOSTON AND NEW YORK.
Trains Leave Either City at . . . .

9.00 A. M. (except Sunday), due at 3.30 P. M.
11.00 A. M. (except Sunday), due at 5.30 P. M.
4.00 P. M. (Daily), due at 10.00 P. M.
11.00 P. M. (Daily), due at 6.40 A. M.

DRAWING ROOM CARS ON DAY TRAINS.   SLEEPING CARS ON NIGHT TRAINS.

For time tables, reservations in palace cars, tickets, or information of any kind,
call on nearest ticket agent, or

A. S. HANSON, Gen'l Pass. Agent,
BOSTON, MASS.

Summary of Classes by States and Countries.

STATES.	'94.	'95.	'96.	'97.	'98.	SPECIALS.
Alabama	—	—	—	1	—	—
California	3	—	—	3	—	—
Colorado	—	—	—	3	—	—
Connecticut	5	4	13	8	1	5
District of Columbia	2	1	4	4	—	3
Georgia	1	—	—	—	—	—
Illinois	4	9	9	10	—	3
Indiana	—	1	—	3	—	1
Iowa	3	2	4	1	2	—
Kansas	1	—	1	3	—	2
Kentucky	1	—	4	2	—	3
Louisiana	—	—	—	2	—	—
Maine	6	6	8	6	1	2
Maryland	—	—	2	1	—	1
Massachusetts	37	43	49	93	2	20
Michigan	—	1	1	5	—	—
Minnesota	1	—	5	—	—	—
CEYLON	—	—	1	—	—	—
INDIA	—	—	—	1	—	—
JAPAN	—	—	—	—	—	1

CONTINUED ON PAGE 29.

T. E. MOSELEY & COMPANY
❀ FINE SHOES ❀

A large assortment for Young Ladies, in all the latest and leading styles, for walking or dress wear. Oxford Ties in Goat, Calf, Kid, Patent Leather, or Russet Color in great variety. Riding Boots a specialty. Prices reasonable. Discount to Wellesley College.

469 WASHINGTON STREET, BOSTON

CUTLER BROTHERS & COMPANY
WHOLESALE IMPORTING AND JOBBING

Druggists and Chemists

NOS. 89 BROAD AND 10 & 12 HAMILTON STREETS

LOWE & REED 1856
REED, CUTLER & CO. 1861

BOSTON, MASS.

MARTIN L. HALL & COMPANY
❀ Wholesale
Grocers

13 AND 14 SOUTH MARKET
33 AND 34 CHATHAM STREETS

A. L. ADAMS
FRED P. ADAMS
CHAS. G. BURGESS

BOSTON, MASS.

BEAUTIFUL LAMPS

Rare Old Delft,
Dresden China,
Terra Cotta,
Antique Silver,
Bright Silver,

Wrought Iron,
Fine Japanese Bronze,
Old Brass,
Ormolu,
Onyx and Cut Glass.

DAINTY CREATIONS IN SHADES TO MATCH.

R. HOLLINGS & CO.,
Importers and Manufacturers

523, 525 WASHINGTON STREET, ...Opposite R. H. White & Co.
BOSTON.

Live and Boiled Lobsters,
Fresh Shad, Blue Fish, Salmon,
Kippered Herring, Soused Mackerel,
Canned Smelts,

QUEEN OLIVES, LIMES,
PLAIN, SWEET, AND FANCY MIXED PICKLES.

All kinds of

RIVER, LAKE, AND OCEAN FISH

Bright, fresh goods; prompt delivery; prices right.

VISIT THE OLD AND RELIABLE

PEOPLE'S FISH MARKET,
Oliver Bros.   SOUTH AVE., NATICK, MASS.

H. BROAD,

CUSTOM SHOE MAKER,

Repairing a Specialty.
Trunk and Skate Straps.

SHOP ON BLOSSOM STREET

NEAR WASHINGTON STREET

WELLESLEY, MASS.

The Wellesley Legenda.

GOWN MAKERS TO WELLESLEY

COTRELL & LEONARD
Cloaks and Furs

MAKERS OF
Caps and Gowns to the American Universities

ILLUSTRATED
MANY ALL ON APPLICATION

ALBANY, NEW YORK
472 and 474 Broadway

J. M. SULLIVAN   D. W. SULLIVAN

GEO. H. CHESSMAN & COMPANY
General Commission and Produce Dealers

No. 21 SOUTH SIDE FANEUIL HALL MARKET

BOSTON

Established in 1870   Branch, 454 Boylston Street
                             Y. M. C. A. Building

ANDREW J. LLOYD & CO.
OPTICIANS,
IMPORTERS AND MANUFACTURERS.

Nos. 323 and 325 WASHINGTON STREET, BOSTON, MASS.

The Wellesley Legenda.

BAILEY'S HOTEL, A. BAILEY, Proprietor.
This hotel is on the line of Boston and Albany R. R., two quarters of an hour's ride from Boston, and is connected by way of coach to Wellesley College, passing the beautiful estate of H. H. Hunnewell. Guests conveyed from depot and College, free of charge. First-class livery stable connected with house. Also, Proprietor of Bailey, Boston Express and Wellesley College Baggage Transfer Co. Telephone connection from depot and College to Hotel. First-class in every respect. Terms reasonable.

PACKER'S TAR SOAP

Is undoubtedly the best Shampooing agent known. It does not dry the hair, but makes it soft and glossy; and is refreshing and beneficial to the hair and skin. Physicians order its use in treatment of Dandruff, Baldness, and Skin Diseases. It improves the complexion.

Summary of Students by Classes.

Seniors	116	Resident Graduates	11
Juniors	124	Candidates for Batchelor's Degrees	666
Sophomores	166	Noncandidates for Degrees	68
Advanced Freshmen	9	Total Number 1893-94	745
Freshmen	251		
Total	666		
	Resident Candidates for higher Degrees	15	
	Nonresident Candidates for higher Degrees	42	

The Wellesley Legenda.

THE WONDER OF HEALING!
CURES
CATARRH, RHEUMATISM, NEURALGIA, SORE THROAT, PILES, WOUNDS, BURNS, AND HEMORRHAGES OF ALL KINDS.

Used Internally and Externally.   Prices, 50c., $1.00, $1.75.

POND'S EXTRACT CO., New York and London.

Furs! Furs!

Jackets, Sacques and Mantles
We show the largest stock in Boston, all our own manufacture, and made in the latest Paris styles.

Our Shoulder Capes are made from all the fashionable furs, and are in all the new styles. We make a specialty of repairing and remodeling Sacques, Jackets and Capes.

 EDWARD KAKAS & SONS, The Leading Furriers
162 Tremont Street, Boston, Mass.

Summary of Classes by States and Countries

CONTINUED.

STATES.	'94.	'95.	'96.	'97.	'98.	SPECIALS.
Missouri	—	5	3	6	—	3
Montana	—	—	1	—	—	
New Hampshire	6	4	11	12	1	2
New Jersey	6	5	11	13	1	—
New York	17	10	15	27	—	9
Ohio	8	7	7	12	—	1
Oregon	—	1	2	1	1	—
Pennsylvania	8	14	4	15	—	4
Rhode Island	3	6	3	6	—	1
South Carolina	—	—	—	—	—	1
South Dakota	—	—	—	2	—	—
Tennessee	—	—	1	2	—	—
Texas	1	—	—	—	—	—
Vermont	2	4	6	7	—	4
Virginia	—	—	—	—	—	1
Wisconsin	1	—	—	—	—	1
NOVA SCOTIA	—	1	1	1	—	—

The Wellesley Legenda.

CAPEN, SPRAGUE & COMPANY

LUBRICATING AND BURNING **OILS** NAPHTHA AND GASOLENE

8 CUSTOM HOUSE STREET, BOSTON.

TRY IT

SAPODONE, FOR THE TEETH
A LIQUID SAPONACEOUS DENTIFRICE

PREPARED AND SOLD BY
OTIS CLAPP & SON, Boston and Providence.

CHARLES W. PERRY,
Apothecary

Pure Drugs and Toilet Articles, Perfumery, Etc.

PARTICULAR ATTENTION GIVEN TO THE COMPOUNDING OF PHYSICIANS' PRESCRIPTIONS.

Shattuck Building

WELLESLEY, MASS.

The Wellesley Legenda.

DOMINICK DUCKETT,

Caterer and Confectioner.

Will give prompt attention to all orders. Skillful and polite attendance furnished. Orders filled at short notice. . . . .

WELLESLEY COLLEGE,

WELLESLEY, MASS.

Ladies' Merchant Tailors.

CUSTOM GARMENTS AT POPULAR PRICES.

Sole Agents for the Famous P. & P. Kid Gloves.

The Most Elegantly Appointed Specialty Cloak House in America for Ladies.

MEDIUM AND FINE GRADE GOODS ONLY.

The Wellesley Legenda.

Exercising Machine. Price, $5.00.

Ladies' Shirts and Blouses. $3.75 and up. Made to special order: **Ladies' Jackets and Skirts.** Entire suits for street wear, outside garments, storm ulsters, waists and blouses. Samples and models now ready at very reasonable prices.

New Shirtings now ready. French Madras, English Oxfords, Scotch Cheviots, and Wash Goods. For men's negligee and outing shirts; for ladies' and children's waists and blouses, or sold by the yard.

Seashore and Country Outfits. Ladies', men's, and boys' negligee shirts, fishing shirts, rowing shirts, bathing suits, ladies' sweaters, men's sweaters, towels and wrappers at **Noyes' Bros.**

Lounging or Blanket Wrap. For the sick room, nursery, bath, steamer traveling, railway carriage, and yachting, for men, women, children, and the baby. $2.75 to $35, with hood and girdle complete. For railway car or steamer traveling they are a positive luxury and comfort. Fifty choice patterns now in stock or made to special order.

NOYES BROTHERS,
Washington and Summer Streets, BOSTON, MASS., U. S. A.

...REFERENCE BOOKS...

Maturin M. Ballou (editor).
A Treasury of Thought. An Encyclopedia of Quotations. 8vo, full gilt, $3.50; half calf, or half morocco, $6.00.
Pearls of Thought. 16mo, full gilt, $1.25; half morocco, $2.50.
Notable Thoughts about Women. Crown 8vo, $1.50.
Edge-Tools of Speech. 8vo, $3.50; half calf or half morocco, $6.00.

Clara Erskine Clement.
Painters, Sculptors, Architects, Engravers, and their Works. A Handbook. With many Illustrations. With Index of Artists, Authors, Amateurs; Chronological Tables of the Principal Painters of the Italian, Flemish, Dutch, German, Spanish, French, and English Schools; with Dates of Birth and Death. 12mo, $3.00; half calf, $5.00; tree calf, $7.00.
A Handbook of Legendary and Mythological Art. With about 175 Descriptive Illustrations. 12mo, $3.00; half calf, $5.00; tree calf, $7.00.

Christian Symbols and Stories of the Saints, as Illustrated in Art. Edited by KATHERINE E. CONWAY. With many full-page Illustrations. Crown 8vo, gilt top, $2.00; half calf, $5.00; full levant, $7.00.
The same. New Edition (not illustrated). Crown 8vo, $1.50.
Stories of Art and Artists. Illustrated. 4to, $4.00; half white vellum cloth, $4.50; half calf, $7.50.

Clara Erskine Clement and Laurence Hutton.
Artists of the Nineteenth Century, and their Works. A Handbook containing 2050 Biographical Sketches. Fully revised. 12mo, $3.00; half calf, $5.00; tree calf, $7.00.

George Willis Cooke.
Guide-Book to the Poetic and Dramatic Works of Robert Browning. Crown 8vo, gilt top, $2.00; when bought in connection with set of Browning's Works, *Riverside Edition*, $1.75.

Sold by all Booksellers. Sent, postpaid, by

HOUGHTON, MIFFLIN & CO., Boston.

The Wellesley Legenda.

HENRY M. BURR & COMPANY

Novelties in Millinery

AT POPULAR PRICES

490 WASHINGTON STREET, BOSTON

Class of Ninety-Four—(Freshman Year.)
   Average Age . . . . . 19 years, 8 months.
   Average Height . . . 5 feet, 3.3 inches.
   Average Lung Capacity . 138 cubic inches.

Class of Ninety-Four Boat Crew—(November, Senior Year.)
   Average Lung Capacity . 150 cubic inches.
   Average Strength of Back . 130.7 pounds.
   Average Strength of Chest . 57 pounds.

..HENRY C. HASKELL..
11 John Street, New York,
DESIGNER AND MAKER.

Society Badges, Fraternity Pins, Rings, Emblem Jewels of every description.
Medals—TROPHIES for presentation, from original and artistic designs.
When you want anything in above line, will esteem it a favor to submit special designs, with estimates, or answer enquiries by mail.
We send design plates FREE upon request.

Wellesley Pins can be obtained from MISS FLORENCE TOBEY, Business Manager of Magazine.

The Wellesley Legenda.

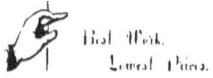 Best Work.　　　　　　　　　Full Count.
　　　　Lowest Prices.　　　　　　　　Prompt Delivery.

Frank Wood, Printer,

No. 352 Washington Street,

Special Attention given to Work　　　Boston.
for Schools and Colleges.

BOOK AND PAMPHLET BINDING IN ALL ITS VARIETIES.

ROBERT BURLEN,

PAPER RULING,

BOOK AND PAMPHLET BINDING,

50 Arch Street and 197 Devonshire Street,

BOSTON.

Special Attention Paid to Binding of Large Illustrated Works, Engravings, etc.
Old Books Rebound, and Folios of Every Description Made to order.

PASSENGER ELEVATOR AT 197 DEVONSHIRE STREET.　　　FREIGHT ELEVATOR AT 50 ARCH STREET.

The Wellesley Legenda.

BAUSCH & LOMB OPTICAL COMPANY
MANUFACTURERS OF AMERICAN STANDARD
PHOTOGRAPHIC LENSES
DIAPHRAGM SHUTTERS
OPTICAL INSTRUMENTS
MICROSCOPES
MAGNIFIERS

OF EVERY DESCRIPTION

FACTORY
ROCHESTER, N. Y.

BRANCH OFFICE
NEW YORK, N. Y.

···H. L. LAWRENCE & CO.···

Wholesale and Retail Dealers in

POULTRY AND GAME

Smoked Tongues and Honey Comb Tripe

STALLS 46 AND 48 FANEUIL HALL MARKET

H. L. LAWRENCE
J. P. LAWRENCE
L. H. HOSMER

BOSTON

The Wellesley Legenda.

GEO. A. PLUMMER & CO.
531 and 533 Washington Street.

Now Open .. The Latest Productions in Ladies' and Misses'

Spring Costumes, Wraps, Coats and Waists.

A Great Variety of Styles from which to make a selection.

ALL AT .... POPULAR PRICES.

MISS NOURSE'S
English and French
Family and Day School.

It has individual advantages for a limited number of family pupils and a full course successfully fitting for leading colleges. A certificate admits to Wellesley.

Walnut Hills,   Cincinnati, Ohio.

HARCOURT PLACE SEMINARY
GAMBIER, OHIO.

MRS. ADA I. AYER-HILLS, B.A., Principal.

This school was founded in 1887 with a Faculty drawn entirely from Wellesley College. College preparatory and finishing courses. An estate of twelve acres. Location of surpassing beauty and healthfulness, in the Episcopal educational center of Ohio. Elegant buildings, tastefully furnished. Superior in its teaching force, and in all its appointments, it was founded to be the most completely equipped and desirable school for girls west of the Alleghany Mountains, and as such invites the attention of the intelligent public.

The Wellesley Legenda.

CHAS. W. HEARN,

·· The Senior Class Photographer of Wellesley College, '94 ··

WOULD respectfully inform all students that by the nature of his contract with the Senior Class, all students and friends of students of said College are entitled to and will receive the finest of photographs, at reduced rates, at his studio in Boston, to which you are invited to call and inspect the specimens on exhibition. Obtain tickets for the purpose of sitting at reduced rates, up to June 20, 1894, of the Senior Class Photo. Committee, MISS ELEANOR S. CHACE, Chairman.

Very respectfully,

392 BOYLSTON STREET, NEAR BERKELEY STREET,   CHARLES W. HEARN,
BOSTON.

J. TAILBY & SON,
..Florists..

OPPOSITE RAILROAD STATION, WELLESLEY, MASS.

Cut Flowers and Plants of the choicest varieties constantly on hand.

Roses, Carnations, Lilies of the Valley, Violets, English Primroses in their season, Bulbs in Variety.

Floral Designs for all occasions, arranged at shortest notice. Orders by mail or otherwise promptly attended to. Flowers carefully packed and forwarded to all parts of the United States and Canada.

An Appeal.

Maidens, give me your attention,
    Listen all to what I say;
I a subject now must mention
    That I've thought on many a day.

Now, you all have noticed, doubtless,
    That our building seems to be
A center of attraction boundless
    For dogs of high and low degree.

But you may not all have pondered
    On each aspect of the case,
When endearments you have squandered
    On favorites of the canine race.

Many of us love the canine,
    Love to see his sportive play;
Having him in recitation
    Helps to while the time away.

Love to see him walk sedately
    Up and down the chapel aisle;
Or parade, with motion stately,
    In the dining room awhile.

But, alas! there'e some among us
    Who the species don't adore;
Do not relish, just at midnight,
    Hearing scratching at the door.

So I earnestly request you,
    That when next a dog you meet,
And desire to show him favor,
    You'll confine it to the street.

The Wellesley Legenda.

THE MERRILL PIANOS
WILL COMMEND THEMSELVES TO THE MOST CRITICAL MUSICIANS.

INSPECTION INVITED.
CORRESPONDENCE SOLICITED.

CATALOGUES FREE
ON APPLICATION.

From the Boston Post...

Among the pianos of the present day commanding marked attention by the best critics, the "Merrill" pianos stand in the front rank.

From the N.Y. ... Musical...

We have...

THE MERRILL PIANO COMPANY, 165 TREMONT STREET, BOSTON, MASS.

BURNETT'S
FLAVORING
EXTRACTS.
We sell no others.
S. S. PIERCE & CO., Boston

ARTISTIC LUNCHES

and how to use BURNETT'S COLOR PASTES; a dainty little book, by Helen Louise Johnson, may be had by sending your name and address to

JOSEPH BURNETT & CO.,
27 Central Street, Boston.

ROYAL BAKING POWDER

—Absolutely Pure.

Highest of all in leavening strength.— U. S. Gov't Report.

The Largest Sporting Goods House in the World.

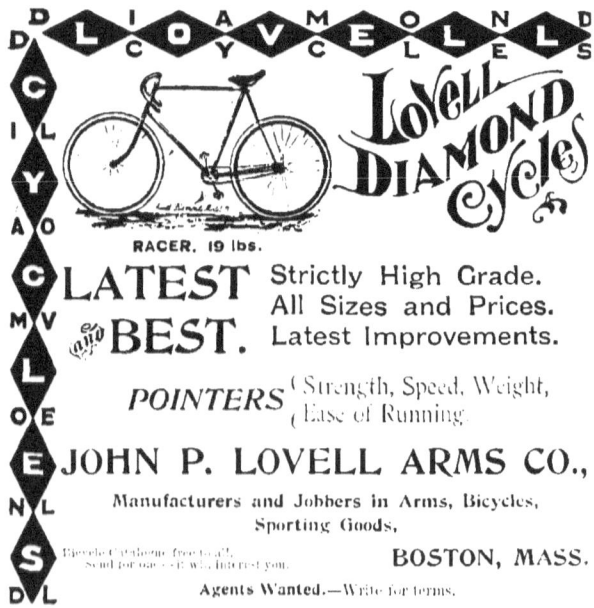

RACER, 19 lbs.

LATEST Strictly High Grade.
All Sizes and Prices.
and BEST. Latest Improvements.

POINTERS (Strength, Speed, Weight, Ease of Running)

JOHN P. LOVELL ARMS CO.,
Manufacturers and Jobbers in Arms, Bicycles, Sporting Goods,

BOSTON, MASS.

Agents Wanted.—Write for terms.

147 Washington Street and 131 Broad Street.

THE BRIDGE TEACHERS' AGENCIES

C. A. SCOTT & CO., Proprietors,

BOSTON AND CHICAGO.

Send for our Agency Manual,

ONE FEE REGISTERS IN BOTH OFFICES.

Offices:
110 Tremont Street,   211 Wabash Avenue,
BOSTON.   CHICAGO.

WE SUPPLY PUBLIC AND PRIVATE SCHOOLS WITH INSTRUCTORS AND

Want Wellesley Graduates

TO KNOW THAT WE CAN HELP THEM . . . . . .

EASTERN TEACHERS' AGENCY,

MISS E. F. FOSTER, Manager,

50 BROMFIELD STREET,

BOSTON.

RICH CUT GLASS.

Our Glass display has long been noted for its

UNRIVALED BRILLIANCY.   PERFECT WORKMANSHIP.

EXCLUSIVENESS OF DESIGN.

Every piece is subjected to a thorough inspection, and nothing is offered for sale that is not ABSOLUTELY PERFECT . . . .

RICHARD BRIGGS COMPANY,

WASHINGTON AND SCHOOL STREETS, BOSTON, MASS.

The Wellesley Legenda.

Isabel Cassidy,

L. K. McGillivrae,

37 and 41 Temple Place,

Boston, Mass.

HIGH-CLASS MANICURE, 50 CENTS.
HAIR-DRESSING IN ALL BRANCHES.
FACIAL MASSAGE.

Good Books
Were never so cheap as now

We make a specialty of carrying the most
Complete line possible of
Books of real value, covering all
Departments of literature

We sell Books at a liberal discount from publishers' prices
Paper-covered Books and Cheap Editions a specialty

De Wolfe, Fiske & Co.
The Archway Bookstore
Nos. 361 and 365 Washington Street, Boston
Send for our Catalogue.

RAYMOND'S VACATION EXCURSIONS.
ALL TRAVELING EXPENSES INCLUDED.
FIFTY-EIGHT SUMMER AND AUTUMN TOURS.

To the principal resorts of New England, the Middle States and Canada, including the White Mountains, Isles of Shoals, Mount Desert, Moosehead Lake, Montreal, Quebec, the Saguenay and St. Lawrence Rivers, Lake St. John, Lake Memphremagog, St. Andrews, St. John, "The Land of Evangeline," Halifax, the Bras d'Or Lakes of Cape Breton Island, Prince Edward Island, the Hudson River, Saratoga Lake George, Lake Champlain, Ausable Chasm, the Green Mountains and the Berkshire Hills, the Adirondacks, the Lehigh Valley, Watkins Glen, Niagara Falls, the Thousand Islands, Trenton Falls, etc.

Excursions to Alaska, outward via the Canadian Pacific Railway, and homeward through the Yellowstone National Park; July 9th and 23d.

Excursions to Colorado, Utah, and the Yellowstone National Park, and also to **Colorado and Return**; July 23d and August 13th.

Excursion to the Yellowstone Park and Return, and also to the **Yellowstone Park and Across the Continent**, returning via California and Colorado; September 3d.

Winter Tours to Mexico, California, the Sandwich Islands, etc.

Fourth Grand Excursion to the Old World.—A Special Train through Central and Northern Europe, with a visit to the Land of the Midnight Sun, the party to leave New York by the North German Lloyd Line, June 20th. Other tours to follow. Send for descriptive book, mentioning the particular tour desired.

RAYMOND & WHITCOMB, 296 Washington Street, opposite School Street, Boston, Mass.

The Wellesley Legenda.

A. B. CLARK  Washington Street, WELLESLEY, MASS.

CHOICE GROCERIES

Fresh Fruits, Nuts and Confectionery.   Canned Goods, Kennedy's Crackers.

All orders will receive prompt attention.--A. B. CLARK.

ESTABLISHED 1818.

BROOKS BROTHERS,
Broadway, cor. 22d St., N. Y. City.
CLOTHING AND FURNISHING GOODS
Ready Made and Made to Measure.

FOR SPRING AND SUMMER OF 1894.

In announcing the opening of the season's goods, we desire to call most particular attention to the fact that we have avoided the present general tendency to reduce stock, and have in no way curtailed ours, either in quantity or variety. On the contrary, we have added several new classes of garments not hitherto obtainable ready made. In style and cut we have endeavored to guard against those exaggerations of fashion so generally found in lower grades of ready made garments.

Our Furnishing Department embraces a most complete assortment of articles in that line for Boys as well as Men. We would call especial attention to a line of leather and wicker goods in this department, including Luncheon Baskets for two, four, six, or eight persons, also Leather Traveling and Kit Bags, Sheffield Plate Flasks, Riding Whips, Crops, etc.

Catalogues, samples, and rules for self-measurement sent on application.

WALNUT HILL SCHOOL,
Wellesley Preparatory,
NATICK, MASS.

Seventeen miles from Boston. Students carefully prepared for Wellesley and other colleges for women.

MISS CHARLOTTE H. CONANT,
MISS FLORENCE BIGELOW,
Principals.

The Wellesley Legenda.

...CHANDLER & COMPANY...

IMPORTERS AND RETAILERS OF

Dry Goods

FINE WOOL DRESS GOODS IN LATEST DESIGNS.

BLACK AND COLORED SILKS,
LADIES' GARMENTS, DUCHESSE GLOVES, PASSEMENTERIES, LACES,
RIBBONS, UNDERWEAR, AND HANDKERCHIEFS.

The newest goods, most reliable qualities, and exclusive styles, always to be found in these departments.

CHANDLER & COMPANY
Winter Street, Boston, Mass.

The Wellesley Legenda.

Willard Hall School for Girls

WAS removed in the summer of 1893 to a new and much more extensive building. It now offers the finest accommodations of any school of this character in New England.

The number of pupils is limited to twenty. Five of the teachers are resident. Music and the modern languages are prominent features.

The School reopens September 18th. Address

Mrs. Sarah M. Merrill
DANVERS, MASS.

A salary of ten thousand dollars a year for a woman teacher would have seemed preposterous a few years ago, yet we can secure it if we can find the woman. The chairman of the nominating committee made personal application to us. "It is not a question of salary," he said, "but of the woman. We would rather pay ten thousand dollars than less if she is worth it." We are not over confident of finding her. We mentioned some of the best women teachers to him. All of them had been considered, and upon one of them the lot might possibly fall. But there were points in which she did not quite meet the ideal of the committee. In fact, the right woman is not now in the front rank. She is doing quiet work in a modest way in some secluded school, and must be **$10,000** why he came to us. It *discovered*. That was the choice must be made from those already known to be good teachers, he wouldn't need to come to an agency. We wish we knew where she is. Perhaps some reader of this can help us. "First a woman, then a lady, then as much more as you can get." All this, of course, this is our old motto, on which our success has been based. But this must be a grand woman such a woman among women as Mark Hopkins was a man among men. And a lady who has or will acquire social distinction—he recognized as pre eminently a lady. And there must be considerable more to get too. Dear, dear, when she has been found it will be easy to say, "Why, of course." But just now we are puzzled. Who will help us find the **WOMAN**

THE SCHOOL BULLETIN AGENCY
C. W. Bardeen, Manager, Syracuse, N. Y.

THE CAMBRIDGE SCHOOL,
Cambridge, Mass.

A PRIVATE School for Young Ladies. Prepares for Radcliffe, Wellesley, Vassar, and other colleges. There are Graduate Courses for young ladies who have finished their work in other schools, but do not care to go to college. There are two Residences, furnishing the comforts of home.

ARTHUR GILMAN, M.A.,
is the Director.

BEACON HILL

STATIONERY STORE.

Special Prices to Students on

Paper, Blank Books, Cards and College Invitations.

Also Stylographic and Fountain Pens.

H. H. CARTER & COMPANY,

3 BEACON STREET, BOSTON.

PET OF THE HOUSEHOLD.

The Wellesley Legenda.

HOWARD SEMINARY.

WELL endowed school for girls. Large and experienced corps of regular and special teachers. Academic and College Preparatory courses, also a special preparatory Course to fit pupils for the regular courses. Certificate of the Principal admits to the Colleges. Thorough training in Classics, Mathematics and English History to prepare pupils well for College.

Excellent opportunity for the study of Music, Art, Elocution, French and German, under teachers who have had exceptional advantages in this country and in Europe.

Careful attention paid to the health of pupils. Buildings large, convenient and well equipped. School building and residence entirely separate. The location is quiet, healthful and accessible, on the Old Colony Railroad, twenty-five miles south of Boston.

For full information send to the Principal.

HORACE MANN WILLARD, D.Sc.,
WEST BRIDGEWATER, MASS.

NorthPacking AND Provision Co. BOSTON, MASS.

PURE LEAF LARD

HIGHEST AWARD
MEDAL AND **DIPLOMAS**
WORLD'S FAIR CHICAGO

FOR PURE LEAF LARD, HAMS, BACON,
DRY, SALTED AND PICKLED MEATS,
BARREL PORK, PURE LARD, SAUSAGES.

FOR SOMETHING EXTRA CHOICE

TRY THEIR **NORTH STAR** BRAND
SURE TO PLEASE.

YOUNG LADIES' JOURNAL
Published Monthly on the 15th day of the month preceding its date.

EACH part contains all the latest Paris Fashions, with Gigantic Fashion Supplement of many figures, and Colored Fashion Plate of twenty-four figures, besides numerous Stories, New Music, New Embroidery Designs, Patterns, etc. Price, 30 cents a copy, or yearly $3.00, including the extra Christmas Number, postpaid. For sale by all newsdealers, and by

THE INTERNATIONAL NEWS COMPANY,
83 and 85 Duane Street,
One Door East of Broadway. NEW YORK.

THE ST. DENIS,

Broadway and Eleventh Street,

Opposite Grace Church,

NEW YORK.

EUROPEAN PLAN

"There is an atmosphere of home comfort and hospitable treatment at the St. Denis which is rarely met with in a public house, and which insensibly draws you there as often as you turn your face toward New York."

LEVILLY & FLECKENSTEIN,

Photo=Engravers.

OUR SPECIALTY,

FINE HALF TONE COPPER PLATES.

7 and 9 State Street,

BOSTON.

My little boy, aged three years, had a severe Cough all Winter, resulting from LaGrippe. For two weeks we did not sleep at night. When the paroxysms came on he had to be held up to keep him from choking to death. Though we had physicians, and the boy took medicine all the time, he never seemed to get any relief until I began to give him Piso's Cure for Consumption. He would sleep several hours after taking a dose. When he began coughing he would halloo "Piso's" as soon as he could get breath. Sometimes I gave him three doses during the night, and after each dose he would go to sleep. We are now giving him the third bottle, and he is so nearly well that a dose taken occasionally is all that is necessary.— Mrs. A. H. SMITH, Bald Knob, Arkansas, April 21, 1893.

Prepared by E. T. HAZELTINE, Warren, Pa.

The Wellesley Legenda.

VALUABLE BOOKS.

Historical Atlas and General History. Royal octavo, 274 pp. of text; 103 Progressive Colored Maps, 70 Genealogical Charts. By Robert H. Labberton. Price, $2.50. Library Edition, half morocco and gilt. Price $3.50. Invaluable to the student of history.
Historical Geography of the United States. 12mo, 41 Colored Maps, with text, by Townsend MacCoun. Price, 75 cents. "The greatest mechanical aid for the study of United States History during a generation."
Institutes of General History. By President E. Benjamin Andrews, D.D., LL.D., of Brown University. Price $2.00.
Principles and Practice of Morality, or Ethical Principles Discussed and Applied. By Ezekiel Gilman Robinson, D.D., LL.D., late President of Brown University. 12mo, cloth, 214 pp. Price $1.25.
The Elements of Psychology. By Prof. Noah K. Davis, of the University of Virginia. Scholarly, critical and exhaustive. Price, $1.35.

For sale by leading booksellers, or mailed by the publishers on receipt of price.

We publish superior text books for all grades of instruction, from the primary school to the university. Our new illustrated Catalogue for 1894 is now ready, and will be mailed free upon application.

SILVER, BURDETT & COMPANY, Publishers,
Boston. New York. Chicago. Philadelphia.

LADIES

The Latest and Most Correct Styles in

MILLINERY

Can always be found at . . . .

THE BOUQUET

134 TREMONT STREET.

MOURNING GOODS A SPECIALTY.

Orders taken at Residences.

STERLING
UNION GARMENTS

In Silk, Wool . . .
Merino and Gauze

Perfection of Fit and Finish.

Equestrian Trousers and
Dress Reform Garments

of all kinds.

The Bates=O'Brien Manfg. Co.
47 Winter Street, Boston.
Catalogue Free. ▼ ▼ ▼ ▼ ▼

FRENCH BOOKS

Readers of French desiring good literature will take pleasure in reading our

Romans Choisis Series, 60 cents vol.
. . . and . . .
Contes Choisis Series, 25 cents vol.

Each a masterpiece and by a well-known author. They are used extensively throughout the country for class-reading, as many have notes in English.

List sent on application ; also complete catalogue of all publications and imported editions of foreign books.

WILLIAM R. JENKINS,

851 and 853 Sixth Ave., 48th St., N. Y.

The Wellesley Legenda.

Telephone, Boston 3343.   Telephone, Brighton 23-3.

NOT THE LARGEST   NOT THE OLDEST
BUT THE BEST.

DREWSEN'S French Cleansing and Dyeing Establishment,
No. 9 TEMPLE PLACE, BOSTON.

All goods returned in one week; earlier if desired. Stage Costumes in one day.
SPECIAL — Curtains and Blankets cleansed to look like new, $1.00 per pair.
Open from 7 A. M. to 7 P. M.

417 Broadway, South Boston.   300 North Beacon Street, Brighton.

ESTABLISHED 1801.

BARRY'S
TRICOPHEROUS

FOR THE HAIR.

The Wellesley Legenda.

E. T. Cowdrey Company,

Preservers and.....
Importers of Table Delicacies

BOSTON.

OFFICE
80 BROAD STREET.

SALESROOM
44 SO. MARKET STREET.

Shattuck & Jones,

DEALERS IN
All Kinds of.... Fresh Fish.

128 FANEUIL HALL MARKET, BOSTON.

An Arthrop Ode.

There was a simple arthropod
    Did sail the summer sea;
They caught him in a lobster pot,
    And brought him home to me.

I cut his little carapace
    About his little gills,
And watched his unsuspecting heart
    Beat soft, subconscious thrills.

I jerked his little walking legs,
    And hewed them, one by one,
From off their basal segments,
    Just as it should be done.

I tore his little systems
    From out his body-wall,
Till of that simple arthropod
    Was nothing left at all.

There's nothing left but diagrams
    Of what he *ought* to be,—
And there's an empty lobster pot
    Upon the summer sea.

    —Florence Converse.

The Wellesley Legenda.

Cloaks and Furs

Messrs. Springer Brothers are always prepared to show a rich and varied assortment of new and stylish CLOAKS of every description, which the young ladies of Wellesley College are cordially invited to inspect.

SPRINGER BROTHERS

 The Cloak Importers and Manufacturers

Fashionable Coats, Jackets, Capes, Silk Waists, Petticoats, Skirts, Fur Capes, Outing, Boating, and Lawn Tennis Suits, etc.

Ladies' Cloaks for Street Wear, Carriage, Railway, and Ocean Travel, for the Opera and other dress occasions.

Latest and choicest European styles and novelties, and elegant garments of Springer Brothers' own celebrated make.

Special Discount to Students and Teachers

Springer Brothers · · ·

Retail and Custom Department

Carriages . . .
10 and 12 Bedford Street.   500 Washington Street, cor. of Bedford Street, BOSTON.

HEADQUARTERS FOR FASHIONABLE CLOAKS AND FURS.

The Wellesley Legenda.

ALBANY TEACHERS' AGENCY

Secures . . . .
Good Positions for
Good Teachers with Good Records.

✿

WE invite competent and well-qualified teachers for all departments of school work, whether experienced or not, to register with us, and pledge our best efforts to advance their interests.

Teachers recommended to school officers without charge. Correspondence invited.

HARLAN P. FRENCH, Manager,

24 State Street   ALBANY, N. Y.

THE FARMER PUZZLE.

Father's Share

Four Sons.

Share of the

Divide in Four Parts equal in size and shape

A solution of this puzzle and a sample of Phenyo-Caffein sent free by the

PHENYO-CAFFEIN Co.

PHENYO=CAFFEIN

✿

is recommended by Physicians for

✿

HEADACHE, NEURALGIA AND
OTHER SEVERE **PAINS.**

Worcester, Mass.

Webster's International Dictionary
The New "Unabridged."

It is the **Standard** of the U.S. Supreme Court, of the U.S. Gov't Printing Office, and of nine-tenths of the Schoolbooks. It is warmly commended by every State Superintendent of Schools.

The One Great Standard Authority.

Hon. D. J. Brewer, Justice of U.S. Supreme Court, writes: "The International is the perfection of dictionaries. I commend it to all as the one great standard authority."

Ask your Bookseller to show it to you
G. & C. Merriam Co., Publishers,
Springfield, Mass., U.S.A.

☞ Send for free prospectus containing specimen pages, etc.
☞ Do not buy cheap photographic reprints of ancient editions.

The Wellesley Legenda.

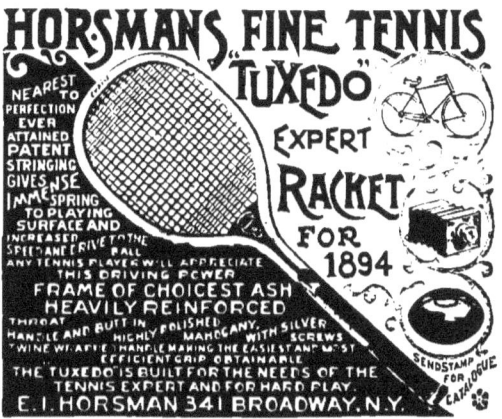

Send the Bride Something

A "Rochester," for instance. One of our handsome Rochester Banquet Lamps will please her; and, in fact, with one of our fashionable silk shades there is more show for the money than anything you can get. The choicest bric-a-brac in the palace of a Vanderbilt reveals nothing finer. We can send you a lamp by express.

SEND TO US FOR OUR ILLUSTRATED CATALOGUE AND PRICES.

The Rochester Lamp Company.

42 Park Place and 37 Barclay Street,

 NEW YORK, N. Y.

"The Rochester" is the name of all that is good and beautiful in a lamp.

The Wellesley Legenda.

THE PLEASURES OF TRAVEL

over the LAKE SHORE AND MICHIGAN SOUTHERN RAILWAY extend to millions of people annually, and it is constantly receiving an increased recognition.

Its reputation for high speed with comfort and safety, its punctual service and elegant equipment, have made the Lake Shore famous and superior as a passenger route between the cities of

Chicago, Toledo, Cleveland, Buffalo, New York and Boston.

ROUTE OF THE
"NEW YORK AND CHICAGO LIMITED."
ONLY 24 HOURS,
CHICAGO TO NEW YORK.

ONLY
DOUBLE TRACK LINE
BETWEEN
BUFFALO & CHICAGO.

...America's Best Railway...

A. J. SMITH, G. P. & T. A., Cleveland, Ohio.

The Wellesley Legenda.

MICHIGAN CENTRAL
"*The Niagara Falls Route.*"

In connection with the

BOSTON & ALBANY
and NEW YORK CENTRAL

forms the route of the

North Shore Limited

and other fast express trains from

BOSTON

AND

New England Points.

Wagner Palace Sleeping Cars of latest design and construction, and unexcelled Dining Car service on all through trains.

∽ ◇ ∽

ROBERT MILLER, Gen'l Supt., Detroit.
    O. W. RUGGLES, Gen'l Pass. and Ticket Agent, Chicago.
        W. H. UNDERWOOD, Eastern Pass. Agent, Buffalo.

The Wellesley Legenda.

THE WONDERFUL WEBER TONE

Is found
ONLY in the

Weber
Pianos

...WAREROOMS...

WRITE FOR ILLUSTRATED CATALOGUE. Fifth Avenue and 16th Street, New York.

...New Mail Cycles...
STRICTLY HIGHEST GRADE.

NEW MAIL,
Ladies' pattern,
$115.
offered as the
easiest frame
for mounting in
the market, also

ATALANTA,
Ladies' pattern
$75.

CHILDREN'S
Wheels $35 up

CATALOGUE SENT ON APPLICATION.

Manufacturers,

WM. READ & SONS,
107 WASHINGTON ST., BOSTON.

Albany Female Academy.
155 Washington Avenue,
ALBANY, N. Y.
FOUNDED, 1814.

A BOARDING and Day School for Girls. Halls and rooms spacious, airy, and attractive. Location unexceled. Buildings heated by steam. Pupils of six years received in the Primary Department. Drawing, French, and German form a part of the three courses of study. Educational equipment of the best. Students prepared for college. Academy certificate accepted at Wellesley. Boarding pupils limited to twenty-five. Home life healthful, refined, Christian.

For catalogue apply to the Principal,
LUCY A. PLYMPTON.
Hon. Wm. L. LEARNED, LL.D., President of the Trustees.

www.ingramcontent.com/pod-product-compliance
Lightning Source LLC
Chambersburg PA
CBHW022106230426
43672CB00008B/1293